Moreschi
The Last Castrato

'For there are some eunuchs, which were so born from
their mother's womb: and there are some eunuchs
which are made of men: and there be eunuchs,
which have made themselves eunuchs
for the kingdom of heaven's sake.'

Matthew xix, 12

Moreschi
The Last Castrato

Nicholas Clapton

HAUS PUBLISHING • LONDON

First published in Great Britain in 2004 by
Haus Publishing Limited
26 Cadogan Court
Draycott Avenue
London SW3 3BX

A CIP catalogue record for this book
is available from the British Library

ISBN 1-904341-77-2 (paperback)

Designed and typeset in Garamond and Futura by Andrea El-Akshar, Köln

Printed and bound by Graphicom in Vicenza, Italy

Front cover: photograph of Moreschi courtesy Lebrecht Music Collection
Back cover: photograph of Moreschi courtesy Fratelli Alinari

Contents

for Eric Southworth

Acknowledgements

My personal thanks for their help and encouragement go to Dr Margaret Bent, Dr Sandro Cappelletto, Prof László Dobszay, Dr Stephen Golding, Dr John Kenyon, Mr Justin Pearson, Dr Sally Prime, Prof Bruce Redford, and Dr Clare Robertson; and to Mrs Diane Forlano, for all her wisdom in matters vocal, and otherwise.

For his tireless patience and assistance I am most grateful to Dr Marco Lauciani, Administrator of the Sistine Chapel Choir. My work was much aided by the Segreteria and Staff of the Vatican Library (for all that, during the period of my research, the Sistine Archives were undergoing a thorough *disinfestazione*), and of the Biblioteca Casanatense in Rome. In that city I was honoured by the warmth and hospitality of Father Ambrose Bennett and other members of the Benedictine community of the Collegio Sant'Anselmo. In Montecompatri my thanks go to the parish priest Father Giovanni Errigo, the Associazione Pro Loco 'Montecompatri 2000', and Signor Franco Gattari.

I also wish to thank the staff of the Bodleian Library, Oxford, especially the indefatigable Dr Peter Ward-Jones and his staff in the Music Reading Room, and Peter Allmond of Inter-Library Loans; the staff of the History Faculty Library of the University of Oxford; and the staff of the British Library Newspaper Division at Colindale.

My greatest debt of gratitude goes to Robert Buning, without whose work on Moreschi my own would have been impossible, and who kindly agreed to my using it as a source of reference, quotation and translation; for my contact with him, I would lastly like to thank the late Elsa Scammell, castrato enthusiast *extraordinaire*, whose web-group about castrati and their history remains a constant source of information and lively discussion.

Foreword

The writing of any biography may be likened to exploring a great lumber-room: in the case of some subjects one may ransack a rich store house of facts, not to mention the conclusions of other writers, picking and choosing one's way to a personal view of the individual concerned. With others, it is more like exploring some long-abandoned, dusty attic by the light of a flickering candle, casting light into dark places, but also maybe creating deeper shadows than were previously present.

For many reasons, the story of 'the last castrato', Alessandro Moreschi, is not an easy one to tell, since his life was indeed one lived largely in the shadows. The whole phenomenon of the castrato has always been hedged about with things likely to make an accurate rendering of its history difficult, if not impossible: fame, glamour, myth-making, squeamishness and guilt (both social and religious) have all had a part to play in this obfuscation. If noticed at all by musicologists, Moreschi himself is generally regarded as an ideal subject for the epithet 'born out of his time', music history's equivalent of the coelacanth or the dodo, a footnote to be regarded, as indeed he was during his own lifetime, with a varying mixture of wonder, curiosity and derision. The truth of the matter is at once more complicated and more interesting, reflecting as it does profound and long-standing uncertainties in human attitudes to sex, morals and gender-roles in society.

Origins and Connections

The vocal tradition of which Moreschi was the 'last' representative stretches back far beyond the famous castrati of seventeenth and eighteenth-century Europe to the vocally-gifted eunuchs of the Imperial Chinese court and the gelded choristers of Byzantium. These in turn derived their very existence from widespread ancient traditions of emasculation, which were presumably first used by humans on male herd-animals in the name of control. The date for their first use on men is lost in the mists of time, and was no doubt originally the rather brutal process of total removal, by a single sword stroke in battle or subsequently as a mark of subjugation or slavery. The Egyptian Pharaoh Merneptah I (reigned about 1234-1214 BC) recorded that he collected 6359 uncircumcised penises from an invading Libyan army, which he had defeated; whether these were harvested from the living or the dead is uncertain.[1]

The institutionalisation of eunuchs as a distinct element in a society is also of early origin. Castration had long been used in ancient China as a substitute for the death penalty, but the first documented appearance of eunuchs at the imperial court dates from the Shang dynasty (1765-1223 BC) when they were known as *huanguan* (after which time the words *huan* and *guan* both meant 'officials' or 'officialdom'). In India, the still-widespread castrato cult of *hijra*, said to derive from an episode in the ancient epic *Mahabharata* in which the great warrior Arjuna dresses as a woman for a year to disguise his masculinity, has always regarded total emasculation as the ultimate expression of asceticism and the renouncing of sexual desire – the operation of total castration is called *nirvan*, an obvious reference to Hindu concepts of higher states of awareness.

It is interesting to note at this juncture the contrasting roles of castrated males in the above two examples. In China, an outwardly male role was retained, and eunuchs often rose to powerful positions at court, whereas in India, the *hijra* are a 'third sex', adopting an outwardly female appearance and living apart from society, with which they interact in a few specific ways, namely as beggars, entertainers and priest(esse)s. This theme of sexual ambiguity is one to which I shall return, as have all writers about castrati.

These two traditions are perhaps the oldest of which we have knowledge, but men were also castrated in ancient Egypt, Mesopotamia, Persia, Greece and Rome, as well as medieval Byzantium and across the Islamic world, though the radical procedure of penectomy plus castration seems by and large to have been confined to the Orient.

Potiphar, to whom the Midianites sold Joseph in the Old Testament story, is described as a eunuch - at least in the Latin Vulgate. In the King James Bible (Genesis, chapter 37, verse 36), the euphemism 'officer' is used, with a note "Heb. *eunuch*: but the word doth signify not only *eunuchs*, but also *chamberlains, courtiers* and *officials*"; quite so.

In China, after removal of the genitalia by one cut of a razor-sharp sickle-shaped knife, the victim's urethra was plugged, the wound dressed with paper soaked in cold water, and all bound tightly. He was then made to walk about for two to three hours before being allowed to lie down. No fluids were permitted for three days, after which the urethral plug was removed. If urine flowed, the operation was regarded as successful. If not, an agonising death would follow.[2] The 'failure rate' was apparently remarkably low.[3] The new eunuch's genitals were then pickled, and returned to him for safekeeping: preserved genitals had to be shown in order to advance in palace hierarchy, and would also be needed in future lives.

The reasons for castration were many and various: as well as subjugation, punishment, service and religion, sexual purposes cannot and should not be ignored. The Roman writer Petronius (27-66 AD) is typically direct in this regard:

> O faeries, O buggers,
>   O eunuchs exotic!
> Come running, come running,
>   Ye anal erotic!
>
> With soft little hands,
>   With flexible bums,
> Come O castrati,
>   Unnatural ones![4]

The obviously derogatory tone of this passage reflects frequently-encountered attitudes of ancient writers to passive homosexual behaviour, but some castrati in some societies were operated on after puberty, (and could therefore perhaps have still achieved an active, erect role). This was the case for instance in the Ottoman Empire, where most if not all castrates were non-Arab, emasculation having been condemned by the Prophet. It has been hypothesised that the employment of eunuchs in harems was not to prevent sexual relations between them and the women they guarded and cared for, but rather merely to ensure that only the ruler could father children on his wives.

The castrati to whom Petronius referred had no option about their physical state, but there have always been men who have chosen or felt a great desire or need for castration. This has a long history in connection with certain religious belief systems: one might mention, in addition to the *hijra,* the ancient cult of the goddess Cybele, early Christian Gnostic ideas relating to spiritual purity, and the Russian Orthodox *skoptsi* sect purged by the Soviets in the 1920s, whose priests were self-castrates. In modern Western society, with the availability of increasingly sophisticated surgical techniques, male-to-female transsexuals are able to achieve a new gender identity, and castration is part of this process.

The cult of Cybele and her followers the Corybantes was of Phrygian origin

The above are concerned with the removal of male sexual organs and/or male sex drive, perceiving them in some way to be undesirable, but castration also has a long history as a means of preserving or creating special positive abilities or qualities. In ancient times castrated slaves were regarded as more docile and controllable (as are geldings, steers, and spayed dogs and cats to this day) and frequently thought of as more faithful to their masters than their whole counterparts. This made them more costly, as did the fact that the procedure was never, in the period before modern medicine, without serious danger of death either from bleeding or, more often, infection.

Castrated men can be classified into three basic types: born eunuchs, who have some endocrinological abnormality preventing puberty and the development of adult male sexual characteristics; those where a radical dismemberment of both penis and testes was employed (corresponding to the ancient Greek *eunochos* and the Roman *castratus,* and the method generally employed in the Orient); and the various forms of 'Western' castrati: the *spado* (*spao* is the Greek for 'extract') involving removal of the testes and epidydimi, the *thlibia* (*thlibo* means 'press') where atrophy of the testes was achieved by exterior kneading or ligation, and the *thlassia*, (*thlao* = 'shatter') where the testes were macerated by a metal or other instrument. This latter was derived from techniques used for the gelding of animals, but all of these methods, let alone the very idea, seem barbarous today, as when castration was achieved during infancy through the kneading of boys' external genitalia by their own mothers or wet-nurses. In the case of young singers it would of course be necessary to wait until their talent had declared itself, but to perform the procedure well before puberty. It is they who are likely to have been placed in a warm bath to 'soften the parts and render them more manipulable and prone to disintegrate' and made insensitive to any pain by pressure on the jugular vein. An alternative was, again after immersion in warm water, to drug the child with opium, 'and when he had been overwhelmed by sleep, those organs which Nature takes so much care to form were cut or torn away.' This latter alternative was regarded as dangerous, since many boys died of an overdose of the narcotic.[5]

In a performance milieu the use of the castrato has by one recent authority been traced to the character of the Phrygian slave in Euripides' *Orestes*, whose hysterical, tragi-comic outpourings (lines 1369-1502) contain several references to eunuchism (Orestes indeed refers to him as 'neither man nor woman';[6] incidentally, the cult of Cybele was also of Phrygian origin). However, it was a combination of specific circumstances prevailing in late Renaissance Europe that led to boys being castrated purely for the sake of preserving their voices in order to make them into public performers, particularly in a secular context.

Within the Christian tradition, castrati had been well-known as singers in the Eastern church from the later years of the fourth century, becoming almost totally dominant, at least in Constantinople, by the early 11th. They were as famed as they were derided for their 'florid and theatrical chanting' (to quote Theodore Balsamon, a late 12th-century Patriarch of Antioch)[7] but their highly-sophisticated singing style largely disappeared after the sacking of Constantinople in 1204 by the Western forces of the Fourth Crusade. It survived only in such Byzantine outposts as Thessaloniki, Epirus, and Italo-Greek monasteries in Sicily, and was never heard again in the capital of the Eastern Empire, even after the restoration of 1261. Thus the musical repertoire of Hagia Sophia from then until the fall to the Ottomans in 1453 was radically different: the castrati had gone, and the new influence in Constantinople of monks trained on Mount Athos, where castrato singers and all other eunuchs were banned and despised, helped to ensure that they never returned. Non-singing eunuchs did, however, remain to a considerable degree in positions of influence at court.

From 1261 to the performance of the first opera (Peri's *La Dafne*) in 1597, by which date castrati had certainly appeared on the scene, is a large gap, and one that has taxed music historians attempting to account for the origins of castrato singing in the West. It has often been attested that the link to the East was through great trading cities, particularly Venice, but recent research has suggested another equally likely route: through the exile of these Byzantine singers to Norman-ruled Sicily. Here King Roger II, though joining in contemporary Western attempts to reduce Constantinople's secular power, nevertheless established at his court in Palermo strictly Byzantine forms of ceremonial, and set up San Salvatore, in Messina, as the mother church of all the Greek cloisters in his kingdom. This would have been an ideal place of refuge for eunuch singers, who formed a tiny but scintillating part of Roger's brilliantly-realised desire to set up cultural and political bulwarks against the Papacy of his time.

From here there may have been links with various ruling houses in Spain (not least that of Aragon which ruled Sicily from 1282), and to the Mozarabic rite of the Spanish Catholic Church. It is likely that the tradition of Spanish falsettists, so often mentioned by musicologists (with the famous 16th-century composer Tomás Luis de Victoria frequently cited as an example) originated with this rite, and also that the Spanish word *falsetista* was at least sometimes used as a euphemism for castrato. Castrati, however high their status or however great their fame, were rarely free of the stigma attached to their mutilated state: the 18th-century Pope Benedict XIV's remark that 'scarcely anyone can be a eunuch without sin'[8] was the least of it. Falsettists, like their present-day counterparts, counter-tenors and male altos, may have been figures of fun for singing in a high, 'woman's' voice, but they were at least 'whole men'. This line of argument may at least provide a link between the ancient and modern castrato worlds.

'Mozarabic' was a term derived from Arabic words meaning 'under Arab control', as much of Spain was during the Middle Ages – the chance of there having been eunuchs in the Moorish courts of Spain also cannot be overlooked.

An anonymous Dutch portrait of Charles V, King of Spain and Emperor of the Holy Roman Empire, with coat of arms and regalia

By the late 1550s there is clear evidence of castrati singing in Italy. They are first mentioned in Rome in 1553 in the *Due Dialoghi della Musica* of Luigi Dentini, a member of St Philip Neri's Congregation of the Oratory.[9] In a letter dated 2 April 1556 the Duke of Ferrara, Alfonso II d'Este, enquires about a castrato he is employing being held up on his way from Savoy.[10]

During the earlier part of the 16th century Spain and the Holy Roman Empire were ruled by the same person, the Emperor Charles V (born 1500; Holy Roman Emperor 1519-1558), who was also related, through his illegitimate daughter Margaret of Austria, to the great Medici and Farnese clans, and thereby to half the noble families of Northern Italy, including the Gonzaga and d'Este. The castrati may thus have arrived in Italy overland from Spain, with fashion-conscious aristocrats vying to employ them.

There were certainly castrati singing in the court chapel in Munich from at the latest 1574, when the great Orlandus Lassus was in charge. It may have been knowledge of this that gave rise to their employment in the Papal choirs, since Giovanni Pierluigi da Palestrina, master of the Cappella Giulia (the choir of St Peter's Basilica in Rome) from 1571 to 1594, would no doubt have been keen to emulate and even surpass his great contemporary. The presence of at least one castrato, Jacomo Antonio Pales (an apparently Catalan surname), in the service of Margaret of Austria, Duchess of Parma, on her estates at L'Aquila, some 60 miles north-east of Rome, is known from correspondence of Cardinal Scipione Gonzaga dating from 1586.[11] Guglielmo Gonzaga, the Duke of Mantua from 1550 and a cousin of the Cardinal, also had a well-attested penchant for castrato singers.[12] In Rome itself, Pope Sixtus V reorganized the choir of the Cappella Giulia in the Bull *Cum pro nostro pastorali munere* dated 27 September 1589, so that it consisted of '12 singers: four basses, four tenors and four contraltos [falsettists], and in addition, for the voice which is called soprano, four eunuchs, if skilled ones can be found; if not, six boys . . . '[13]

The first named castrati of the Pope's private chapel (the Sistine) were Pietro Paolo Folignato and Girolamo Rossini, both admitted in 1599, though it seems likely that others had been enrolled earlier, hidden behind the falsettist designation. In this regard, the 'status' of the Spaniard Francisco Soto, appointed in 1562, is uncertain, although he too was probably a castrato, not least since he taught the first famous castrato of the 17th century, Loreto Vittori. A note from the Vatican Archives about a singer recruited in 1571 certainly shows that by that date castrati were no longer rare or strange creatures: 'Johannes Paredes [a Spanish surname], he is a castrato and has been appointed because there is a need for sopranos. He does not have a very good voice but he can be kept on while we wait for the arrival from Spain of other sopranos.'[14] It is worth noting that this document, like Sixtus V's Bull, implies that not all castrati were good singers: this is hardly surprising. Perhaps their novelty value and the maybe prurient fascination they held for some people outweighed, on occasion, purely aesthetic considerations (a phenomenon concerning singing that continues to this day). Nor were these first castrati necessarily better than their more-established falsettist counterparts, but their new voices rapidly found general favour and the accolade of papal sanction: Pope Clement VIII (reigned 1592-1605), remarked: 'the creation of castrati for church choirs was to be held *ad honorem Dei* ('to the honour of God').'[15]

Clement VIII, generally held to have been an astute man, was clearly also something of a sensualist. On another occasion, when presented with a demand from the clergy of Rome for that newly-arrived drink coffee to be banned, he said: 'This Satan's drink is so delicious that it would be a pity to let the infidels have exclusive use of it. We shall cheat Satan by baptising it.'

Pope Clement VIII and Charles V arrive in Bologna for the Emperor's coronation; painting by Juan de la Corte

Clement was only the most eminent of his contemporaries to prefer the power and brilliance of the castrati to the reedier and thinner timbre of the falsettists, and they also clearly outshone the comparatively transient beauty of boys' voices. The flexibility of the castrato instrument also made it an ideal vehicle for the performance of late 16th-century Catholic church music, which often involved melismatic ornamentation of the comparatively plain written vocal lines. This was in clear contradiction of the reforms of the Council of Trent, which had closed in 1563: 'all should be pronounced clearly and distinctly, and make its way undisturbed into the hearts and ears of the listeners . . . it should have nothing profane intermingled with it . . . '[16] [see also sidebar on p 91]. This battle between religious propriety and what might be termed 'vocal profanity' has continued more or less to the present day (it is curious that, in a spirit of modernisation, many Christian churches today have welcomed pop music idioms, without worrying about their profane connotations). In any case, the *falsettisti* never made the

transition to the opera stage, and in Italy they rapidly faded away: the last soprano falsettist in the Sistine Chapel choir, Giovanni de Sanctos, died in 1625.

Castrati, in contrast, were not confined to the churches for long. The newly-developed form of opera and its attendant monodic musical forms were to provide the essential springboard for them as public performers.

Monody is a type of vocal composition setting a detailedly expressive solo line, supposedly imitating speech patterns, over an instrumental bass-line called a *basso continuo*; it was developed in Italy during the late 16th century and was intended to form part of a recreation of classical Greek drama; it is in total contrast to earlier forms of imitative, polyphonic vocal music, in which each line is ideally of essentially equal importance.

The score for Peri's *La Dafne* (see p 6), is lost, but in 1600 there was performed in Florence the same composer's opera *Euridice* (a version of the archetypally musical legend of Orpheus) in collaboration with his famous contemporary Giulio Caccini. The cast-list for the first performance included three castrati, two of them singing female parts. This work was written for the marriage in Florence of King Henry IV of France to Maria de Medici.

While natural high male voices, namely tenors, continued to be prominent in opera for a while, there was an increasing trend for 'castrato' to become equated with 'leading man'. This convention was firmly entrenched by the 1680s, by which time opera was popular throughout Europe. The castrati became the pop-stars of their day. Few 'normal' singers, male or female, ever came close to matching their fame and success, while reports and anecdotes abound of their vanity, temperament, sexual adventures and fabulous wealth, in addition to general amazement at their vocal gifts or sneering at their indifferent acting. For almost two centuries across Europe (with the notable exception of France) their voice was law.

As has so often been the case throughout history, the rise of the castrato singer may essentially be put down to fashion and that unquenchable human desire for something different. Also, within the rigid social hierarchies of that time, the high pitch of his voice would have carried suitable connotations of elevated social status, while his apparent renunciation of sexual fulfilment would reflect ideas of the desirability of celibacy, which, though dating from early Christian thinking, were by no means extinct even by the late 17th century. There were also economic elements at work: in the context of general European crisis brought about by such events as the Thirty Years' War (1618-1648), celibacy in Italy was on the increase. For the rich, setting up a child in the Church was cheaper than obtaining secular preferment, while for the less well-off, any member of the family in the comparatively safe harbour of ecclesiastical life was simply one less mouth to feed. It was also a method of birth control in troubled economic times. Though voluntary celibacy and castration should by no means be confused, one French traveller to Italy at this time felt able to remark that the latter 'attracts no notice in a country where the population is huge in relation to the amount of work available'.[17] Monks were also referred to as 'unoperated castrati . . . '.[18]

Extraordinary though it may seem to modern sensibilities, there are even well-documented cases of boys desiring to be castrated in order to save their voices: 'Silvestro Prittoni, servant of Your Serene Highness, finding himself in the state of rejoicing in a voice sufficiently good to practise music and wishing to retain it, begs Your Serene Highness in his goodness to make it such that he is without those instruments, which would allow the change of voice to take place with advancing years; that he might receive all this as charity, it being the case that he cannot find the means of being able to do this because of his poverty' (petition to the Duke of Modena granted 11 May 1687).[19] It had nothing necessarily to do with poverty at all: Gaetano Majorano (1710-1783), later famous as the castrato Caffarelli, was granted the income from two vineyards belonging to his grandmother at the age of ten 'that he might profit from the study of grammar and also give attention to Music with the utmost propriety, towards which the said Gaetano is said to have a large inclination, desiring to be castrated and be made a eunuch'.[20]

Portrait of Fernando Tenducci by Thomas Gainsborough

The Catholic Church, having been one of the first Western establishments to employ castrati, was nonetheless always in a quandary about them. In Canon Law castration, along with other forms of mutilation, was punishable by excommunication, though in the 17th and 18th centuries the Pope, as temporal ruler of the Papal States, went along with other harsh contemporary penal codes in Italy in using mutilation as a punishment for criminals.

The Church's rules against castrati marrying were ruthlessly enforced, since they obviously could not procreate. On hearing that one of the Sistine castrati had made one of ladies of the papal court pregnant Pope Alexander VII (reigned 1655-67) remarked 'che si castri meglio' ('let him be castrated better').[21] There is an enormous amount of anecdotal evidence about castrati as lovers of all inclinations, but in exactly which way they were 'active' is still a matter of controversy. (Some recent research on men with the condition of congenital bilateral anorchia, which closely imitates pre-pubertal castration, seems to indicate that more or less normal sexual activity was possible for castrati.)[22]

There were occasional instances of castrati marrying, the most notorious example being Fernando Tenducci (1736-fl 1800), who eloped with and married, in a Protestant ceremony, a Miss Dora Maunsell of Limerick. Prosecuted by her family (she was a judge's daughter) poor Tenducci was thrown into prison. Eventually reunited with his wife, he surprised everyone by fathering two children. As he told Casanova: 'Nature made me a monster to keep me a man'. According to the singer, he was a 'triorchis', and his castration had removed only two of his three seminal glands.

Another source of difficulty arose from the ancient tradition, dating back at least to Tertullian and St Augustine, that disapproved of women appearing on the stage, where they were associated with all forms of licentiousness and prostitution. However, their necessary replacement in opera by castrati dressed as women could hardly be seen as morally superior. Outside the Papal States, women often sang on stage, but even where the Papacy had temporal jurisdiction, successive pontiffs vacillated between enforcing the ban and not. Attempts were even made to ban castrati completely, but the fashion for them was too strong. Benedict XIV's treatise *De dioecesana synodo*[23] of 1748 (a huge, multi-volume work concerned with ecclesiastical governance) is generally disapproving of the whole castrato phenomenon, but this pope at least also realised the limits of his and the Church's power in the face of popular taste. He feared a fall in congregation numbers had bishops attempted to remove these singers and the theatricality that attended them, which was a clear attractant to worshippers. To see an element of hypocrisy in all this is inescapable, and recently there have been calls for the Pope to make an official apology for the Church's use of castrati, though how much this reflects present-day 'holier than thou' moralising is certainly disputable.

By the later 18th century the prevailing social climate in Rome seems to have been liberal, to say the least, so perhaps it is not surprising to find Giacomo Casanova, the notorious libertine, taking a distinct interest in castrati. He describes one, 'the favourite pathic [catamite] of Cardinal Borghese', as having 'a breast as beautiful as any woman's; it was the monster's chiefest charm . . . to feel nothing one would have to be as cold and impassive as any German'. He goes on to discuss the relative proprieties of bedding women and castrati with a distinctly lascivious abbé who 'was an avowed partisan of the forbidden fruit.'[24] Casanova also famously had an affair with a castrato called Bellino, who turned out to be a woman in disguise! Secular society just chose to ignore what we perceive as a barbarous practice for the sensual rewards, of all kinds, to which it could give rise. With this in mind, it is no wonder that the English music-historian Charles Burney wrote: 'I inquired throughout Italy at what place boys were chiefly qualified for singing by castration, but could get no certain intelligence. I was told at Milan that it was at Venice; at Venice, that it was at Bologna; but at Bologna the fact was denied and I was referred to Florence; from Florence to Rome, and from Rome, I was sent to Naples. The operation most certainly is against the law in all these places, as well as against nature; and all the Italians are so much ashamed of it, that in every province they transfer it to some other.'[25]

———

In music, as in all walks of life, tastes and fashions change. Of the many thousands of boys castrated in Italy for the sake of a possible great singing career and its attendant wealth and fame, only a few hundred 'made it'. If their voices survived adolescence at all, which could never be guaranteed, many of the remainder found employment in churches, adapting the latest operatic hits to sacred words. A few perhaps, as a result of their rigorous training, found alternative careers in secular theatre, while some no doubt turned to prostitution to survive.

The reasons for the decline of the castrati are often laid at the door of operatic reformers like Christoph Willibald von Gluck (1714-1787). From his *Orfeo ed Euridice* of 1762 onwards, his operas show a clear desire to break with the stylised floridity of *opera seria*, which had previously been utterly dominant, and had become the perfect vehicle for the castrato's art. However, Gluck still wrote the lead role of Orfeo for a castrato, Gaetano Guadagni, a singer who had earlier worked for Handel, and who was famous for achieving great musical and emotional effects by the simplest of means, rather than by dazzling his audiences with show-off displays. Many of Gluck's later operas were written for Paris, where he did not have the option of writing for castrati, but his reforms did not affect mainstream contemporary opera composition in Italy to the extent of excluding entrenched Metastasian conventions, many of which were in use in serious Italian opera at least until the time of Rossini. An increase in the popularity of comic opera is also cited as a reason for the castrato's fall from grace, but this is hardly more convincing, since some of them were well-known as singers of *opera buffa*. Guadagni, for example, began his career as a *primo amoroso* ('first lover', the equivalent of 'romantic lead') with one such company.

Pietro Trapassi, known as Metastasio (1698-1782), was the most famous librettist of the Italian Baroque operatic form known as *opera seria*, his theatrical works being in a strict classical tradition, with rigid conventions of dramatic structure, poetic metre, and the like. He was a close friend of the great castrato Carlo Broschi, called Farinelli.

It would seem rather that historical coincidence had as large a part to play in the decline of the castrati as in their meteoric rise. Because of a general economic revival in Italy, which began about 1730, parents would have seen improving prospects for their sons and more varied opportunities for advancement – there was a noticeable falling-off in monastic vocations at this period, for example. The Napoleonic wars, which ravaged much of Europe from about 1798 until 1815, played havoc with social and artistic structures in Italy, including the conservatoires where young castrati had received their rigorous training. Such an educational strictness may in any case not have appealed to young singers in the then prevalent atmosphere of revolution and republicanism. Those parts of Italy under French rule during this period adopted the *Code Napoléon* of 1804, which, amongst many other laws, enshrined the long-held Gallic prejudice against castration in a legal framework. The papal ban against women appearing on stage also had no place under French law and tradition, and was rescinded. Ironically Napoleon himself was completely enraptured by the singing of the castrato Girolamo Crescentini, whom he first heard in Vienna in 1805 after the French conquest of that city. The Emperor made Crescentini a Knight of the Iron Cross of Lombardy, awarded him a state pension and invited him to Paris, where he remained until 1812. No doubt some of the Emperor's contemporaries would have derided his taste while consoling themselves by remembering that he was, after all, a Corsican.

This was perhaps one of the last conquests that a castrato ever made, at least theatrically speaking. Within a few short years of the disruption of the conservatoire tradition, the supply of castrati for Italian opera houses began to dry up. The great Luigi Marchesi, born in 1754, had retired in 1806, and with Crescentini in France, the only castrato of the first rank performing on stage was Giovanni Battista Velluti, who, born in 1781, was just old enough to have completed most of his training by the

Portrait of Metastasio by Rosalba Carriera

time of the first French invasion of Italy in 1798. Of course, one singer could not be everywhere, and already by the 1809-1810 season composers in Florence and Naples, who had no option but to continue writing operas, were writing the role of 'first man' for female sopranos (and indeed still calling them *primo uomo*). Rossini wrote a leading role in his opera *Aureliano in Palmira* (1813) for Velluti, who also had the honour of being the last castrato to appear on the operatic stage (in Meyerbeer's *Il Crociato in Egitto* of 1824). By this time, people were becoming quite as accustomed to seeing women singing men's leading roles as they had been used a hundred years earlier to castrati ravaging hearts

Allegorical portrait of Farinelli (Carlo Broschi) by Jacopo Amigoni c 1735

by the exposure of their ample bosoms in female parts, though it is hard to explain why that fine contralto Marietta Alboni's appearance as Prince Arsace in Rossini's *Semiramide* sporting a false moustache (in 1847!) was really any less ridiculous a sight than that of the incomparably great castrato Farinelli singing as one Adelaide (dressed in yards of silk and lace) in his teacher Nicola Porpora's opera of that name premiered in 1723.

Gilbert-Louis Duprez, an engraving 1830

Pace the great contraltos of that period (and indeed of more recent times), even in the exotic operatic world such cavortings *en travesti* could not satisfy in all dramatic situations. From a musico-dramatic perspective, an important factor in the castrato's demise was the fundamental change that took place in 'real' tenor voices during the 1830s. The castrato sound, so new in the 16th century, was to be finally forced out in its turn; the *coup de grace* was administered by Gilbert-Louis Duprez (1806-1896), the first 'king of the high Cs'. After training in Paris, Duprez was dissatisfied with his modest early successes at the Théâtre de l'Odéon, and so in 1828 began an eight-year sojourn in Italy. While there he met the well-known tenor Domenico Donzelli, who had discovered that, by consciously lowering the larynx, a darker and more powerful type of tenor sound could be produced. High notes, including the notorious top C, were now available in full 'chest' voice, and this technique has continued to be used by some operatic tenors to the present day.

Imitators of Duprez' technique of the *voix sombrée* (darkened voice) have often paid for it in shortened careers blighted by a wobbly sound - many singing-teachers still consider the forceful lowering of the larynx unnecessary and indeed dangerous, smacking of artificiality and forcing. It is certainly not necessary to hold the vocal mechanism down to produce powerful high notes: the human larynx floats in a complex system of muscles and ligaments, which, with correct use of the breath, can achieve remarkable results without pushing and shoving – listen to Caruso, Pavarotti or Corelli!

Previously tenors, in the top third or so of their range, seem to have sung in a much gentler, mixed register (perhaps sounding rather like a good modern counter-tenor), which had permitted them to sing extremely high, if comparatively lightly. There were exceptions: the famous Irish singer Michael Kelly, who created the roles of Basilio and Don Curzio in Mozart's *Le Nozze di Figaro* (1786), astonished his hearers by singing to high A in full chest voice. He may not have reached Duprez' dizzying heights, but also did not resort to possibly dubious technical means to arrive *in excelsis*. It is an interesting fact of vocal pedagogy that the small interval of a minor third between A and C can feel huge to both singer and teacher.

The first public response to Duprez was one of stupefaction: even Hector Berlioz, a great composer alive to all musical extremes, was not completely sure of his own reaction: ' . . . this daring artist threw out in chest voice, accenting each syllable, several high notes which possessed a vibratory force, a heart-rending sadness of expression and a beauty of sound, of which nothing previously heard had given the least notion. An amazed silence filled the room, everyone holding their breath, with surprise and admiration mixed in a feeling close to fear . . . .'[26]

His older contemporary Rossini, brought up in an earlier Italian tradition, described the sound as 'the cry of a capon when you strangle it', but the public were soon enraptured with the new, unashamedly masculine timbre and Duprez' whole style of singing, which swept all before it. Duprez had a great success in Rossini's *Guillaume Tell* in 1837, his debut at the Paris Opéra, eclipsing the memory of his rival Adolphe Nourrit, who had created the role of Arnold at that opera's first performance in 1829. In 1836, Nourrit had resigned from the Opera while at the height of his powers, probably ill at ease that the management, no doubt only thinking of box-office receipts, had engaged him and Duprez at the same time. Nourrit kept to the technique of the 'old school', rather than sacrificing everything to the excitement of jangling chandeliers and rattling rafters. His pride was obviously stung by his rival's success, and he fell prey to depression, fearing that his singing days were numbered. He even attempted to imitate Duprez' technique, but it exhausted him. In February 1839, after a great success in Naples as Pollione in Bellini's *Norma*, he committed suicide by hurling himself from the top floor of his lodgings.

This tragic event may also be regarded as bringing down a significant curtain in operatic history. Nourrit heard Velluti sing in Venice in 1837, by which time the castrato was well into his fifties and retired. The tenor must therefore have requested their meeting, and is known to have admired the older singer's technique, not least because their approach to the high register would have been very similar (apparently the castrati did not, on the whole, 'blast' on their top notes, unlike some today who would imitate them).[27] One can hardly imagine such a meeting of minds between Velluti and the macho-sounding, stentorian Duprez. It is ironic that Duprez reported in his own memoirs that he himself narrowly avoided castration, only being saved from his teachers' wishes by the direct intervention of his father.

Velluti died in 1861, operatically the last of his line, but just three years previously a child had been born who would carry the extraordinary castrato sound into the candle-lit shadows of churches and the brittle glitter of Roman salons for another fifty years.

Beginnings

'In the year of Our Lord 1858, on the 11th day of
November, <u>Moreschi</u> Alessandro Nilo Angelo, born on
the said day at 11 o'clock, of the lawfully married spouses
Luigi Moreschi, son of the late Francesco [Moreschi] and
of the late Antonia Carrari, and Rosa Pittoli, daughter of
the late Giuseppe [Pitolli] and Antonia Salvatori, was
baptized by me, Pietro Moreschi, acting for the parish
priest, in the Church here; and I was the godfather, with
the godmother, Signora Agnese Fortunati of Rome,
daughter of Nicola [Fortunati] and Francesca Martucci.
Midwife: Teresa Pagliari. It is so.'

Thus reads the entry for Alessandro Moreschi's birth in the
register of Santa Maria Assunta, the parish church of
Montecompatri.[28] He was the sixth child and younger son of his
parents: his typically long-suffering mother bore eight children in
21 years, all delivered by the indefatigable Signora Pagliari.[29]

Montecompatri is a small hill-top town, some five miles east
of Frascati, in the area known as the *Colli Romani*. To this day the
narrow and steeply-sloping cobbled streets of the old town retain
a powerful atmosphere of the past. Walking up to the Duomo of
Santa Maria Assunta from the bustling Piazza Garibaldi there is
a noticeable quietness on which the occasional motor vehicle
intrudes oddly, while the panoramic views from this ancient
citadel seem little changed by the modern world.

Montecompatri: the Fontana dell'Angelo and Piazza
Garibaldi – in a late 19th-century photograph

Luigi Lorenzo Moreschi and Rosa Maria Pitolli married on 20 December 1841; their children were: Maria Teresa (born 16 April 1843), Sofia Marguerita (29 August 1845), Ieronimo Vincenzo (5 May 1848), Irene Josefa (14 March 1850), Altemia Leonilde (2 April 1852), Alessandro Nilo Angelo (11 November 1858), Gwendolina Nazarena Monica (1 March 1862), and lastly Giulia Secundina (1 May 1864).

The town, founded sometime in the late 11th century, was the possession of several noble Roman families in turn, especially the Colonna and Borghese. After the Napoleonic wars, Montecompatri came under direct Papal control. In 1863, when Moreschi was five, the population was 2,259. Though only about 20 miles from the capital, Rome would still have felt distant, since there was no railway station nearer than Frascati. Pope Pius IX (and no doubt many of his subjects) regarded the railway as the work of the devil, and had not sanctioned this first line in his dominions until 1856; rail travel had arrived in the Italian peninsula 17 years earlier. Thus mule or horse and cart were still the main mode of transport in the area, which was, in any case, by no means advanced in socio-economic terms. At the 1871 census 67.7 percent of the population of the region of Lazio was illiterate, while agriculture was inefficient (average land yield was about a third that of Britain), and, in rural areas particularly, the diet was poor, being based on bread, beans, onions, salt, lard and oil. To the young Alessandro vegetables were probably every bit as much of a luxury as wine and meat. He would, however, have attended the local elementary school, and in this he was very fortunate, since two years of primary education did not become compulsory in Italy until 1877 - even then the law was by no means rigorously enforced, usually through a lack of money.

With hindsight, an event of significance in the singer's young life occurred on 12 August 1865, when the Pope visited

Montecompatri from an early 19th-century engraving

Montecompatri. This was not such an unusual event in itself, since the town was the home of an image that had long been an object of veneration for popes and prelates, as well as local people: the *Madonna del Castagno* ('Madonna of the Chestnut Tree').

Housed in a small church on the hill below the local monastery of San Silvestro, this holy picture of the Virgin and Child seems to have arrived there during the second half of the

School would probably also have been where Moreschi met with standard Italian for the first time. At the time of his birth, dialects were lingustically dominant throughout Italy. King Vittorio Emmanuele always spoke Piedmontese, even to his ministers, while in 1871, out of a population of 26.8 million, it is estimated that only about 2.5% spoke the 'literary' language. The inhabitants of Montecompatri are still proud of their dialect to this day, publishing articles in it in the local monthly journal *Controluce*.

16th century. Having originally been founded as a Franciscan convent, San Silvestro became Papal property in 1532. In 1541 Pope Paul III declared it a *Commenda* (monastic benefice given in trust) 'for the enjoyment of high ecclesiastic dignitaries', the first being Cardinal Uberto Gambara (1489-1549), who took charge of the place, accompanied by numerous courtiers, *litterati* and other friends. The image, painted on wood, was originally placed in an oratory designed for the private devotions of Gambara's many clerical visitors, the Pope included, but it rapidly became an object of local and wider adoration and pilgrimage.

However, the status of San Silvestro was soon to change. In 1587, Pope Sixtus V made it an abbey and by 1603 it had become a house of Discalced Carmelite Friars. They, as an enclosed order, were faced with the problem of what to do about the Madonna, since popular devotion and the preservation of the peace of their enclosure were hardly compatible. Their solution was to place the picture on the stump of a chestnut tree on the boundary of their land, surrounding it with a wooden shrine. In about 1680 this was replaced with the still-existing stone chapel, with separate entrances for the monks, and pilgrims or other worshippers. Locally there is also a tradition that the friars tried to prevent the populace from venerating the image, turning a crowd away from the monastery. The next day a woodcutter saw it translated miraculously into the branches of a chestnut tree, to which it

The monastery of San Silvestro (upper right); the chapel of
the Madonna del Castagno is just visible through
the trees at the left of the photograph.

returned even when the Carmelites tried to retrieve it.

It was in this little chapel, seating only a few dozen and situated
more than a mile outside the town, that Moreschi himself said he
sang as a boy,[30] rather than at his local parish church. This seeming
oddity can probably be explained by suggesting that he performed
there as a soloist on high feast days only, as well as in the town
church. It may have been on one such occasion that a priest or
cardinal from Rome heard him and noted his talent. What he sang
is unknown, but it should be remembered that Gounod's
'Meditation on a Prelude of Bach', known to us as 'the Bach/Gounod
"Ave Maria"', was already well-known by the 1860s.[31] Moreschi's
famous recording of this piece in later life may well have been an
expression of nostalgia for his childhood performances.

This chapel was also the focus of one of the most extraordinary
events of young Alessandro's life. In the summer of 1867 a cholera
epidemic swept through the Colli Romani, but Montecompatri

The original image of the Madonna del Castagno was stolen on 2 December 1919, but a copy was made in 1920, and, blessed by Pope Benedict XV, still draws the faithful. To this day an annual festival is held in the Chapel of the Madonna del Castagno on the first Sunday in September, at which the *monticiani* give thanks to the Virgin Mary for bringing the cholera outbreak to a sudden and miraculous end. The more rational explanation for the cure is that Montecompatri was fortunate enough in the 19th century to have had a clean and reliable fresh water supply from the Tufello spring.

was saved, it is said by the intercession of the Virgin, the whole town having gone in procession to pray to the Madonna del Castagno.

As was the case with nearly all castrati, no written records survive of how or why Moreschi was gelded, and he himself was understandably reticent on the subject. Childhood accidents had often been used as excuses for having boy singers castrated, and the nearest to an explanation ever given for Moreschi's state followed this line: a source at the Pontifical Institute of Sacred Music gave the reason as 'a never thoroughly understood childhood mishap . . . '.[32]

This 'mishap' could have happened shortly after birth. He was the only one of his family to have been baptised on the day he was born, which implies that he was in imminent danger of death. Castration of infants was sometimes invoked as a life-saving procedure, and he probably remained a sickly child. From this hypothesis it follows that his having a fine singing voice as a boy was merely a fortunate coincidence. However, the 1867 cholera epidemic could also have been significant. Castration had for centuries been cited as a cure for illnesses as varied as gout and hernia, for both children and adults, and this practice was not unknown in 19th-century Italy. It may, therefore, have been used on Alessandro to save him from a disease which had terrified Europe for centuries, the coming of which could have provided a pretext for preserving his voice.[33] Moreschi spoke proudly of being permitted to sing solos in the Castagno chapel, and it is more than possible that he did so during the townspeople's supplications to the Virgin, with rumours of his talent reaching Rome along with the whole miraculous story. He

The chapel of the Madonna del Castagno

was only eight years of age at the time of the cholera outbreak – well before puberty, and the perfect time for the operation.

By such a route Moreschi could also have taken what was a traditional path to castration, since he himself, many years later[34], named the person responsible for his leaving home to further his musical training in Rome: Nazareno Rosati (1817-1877), a Minorite friar, who had been a member of the Sistine Chapel choir from 1841 until 1866. He had sung both contralto and tenor, but had retired early because of vocal problems, and turned his attention to teaching and composition. By this time he seems in addition to have been acting as a scout for likely new voices. Moreschi names him as his first teacher, so it may have been Rosati who persuaded Alessandro's parents that their son's voice was of such quality that it should be preserved (many castrati of earlier times were said to have been gelded at the prompting of their teachers). How he may have managed this is not known: to the modern mind their agreement to such a thing is almost inconceivable. Nor does Moreschi speak of Rosati through clenched teeth - if the latter was responsible for Alessandro's condition, his victim seemingly bore him no ill-will.

It is, of course, a matter of coincidence of birth, both in time

The Risorgimento had begun after the Congress of Vienna in 1815, which finally ended the rule of Napoleon over large tracts of Europe, and was a long and frequently bloody struggle for the unification of Italy that lasted until 1870, involving conflicts with several of the Great Powers of Europe, particularly France and Austria. Giuseppe Garibaldi (1807-1882) was the movement's most famous military leader; Giuseppe Mazzini (1805-1872) had been dictator of the Roman Republic of 1848, while Camillo Benso, Conte di Cavour (1802-1861) had become a prime mover of the Risorgimento while prime minister of the Kingdom of Sardinia from 1852.

and place, that made Moreschi's castration in any way possible. For all that events in the wider world seem not have impinged on the seclusion and the quietude of Montecompatri, the Risorgimento, led by such figures as Mazzini, Garibaldi and Cavour, and the movement towards unification in Italy which arose from it, were moving towards their triumphant conclusion.

Within a year of Alessandro's birth, the Papal States had been shorn of the larger part of their territory, losing Umbria, the Marches and Romagna to the Italian state. Only the original 'Patrimony of St Peter', an area somewhat smaller than that of modern Lazio, remained under the Pope's temporal jurisdiction, but this did include the diocese of Frascati in which Montecompatri is situated.[35] *Castratio euphonica*, as the preserving of boys' voices in this manner was later termed, may have become exceedingly rare and socially frowned upon, but it was not made officially illegal in this part of Italy until the capture of Rome by anti-papal forces in 1870, and the adoption of a French-style penal code throughout the country.

Early Days in Rome

By 1870 the only possible place to live and work for a young man in Moreschi's state was Rome, and his only possible employer the church. Thus it was inevitable that he should leave his quiet existence in the Colli Romani and come to the Eternal City. His arrival there in 1871, under the tutelage of Rosati, could hardly be said to have been well timed, since his potential employer, Pope Pius IX, was in an embattled position, to say the least, experiencing the final triumph of the Risorgimento by being the first Pope for over a thousand years without temporal sovereignty.

Just a few months before, Rome's ageless grandeur had been considerably buffeted by the onslaught of the army of the Italian state, though the fall of the city, on 20 September 1870, was in the end rapidly achieved. His ears still ringing with the debates of the First Vatican Council, which had proclaimed the doctrine of Papal Infallibility as recently as 18 July, Pius IX was angered and insulted by his loss of worldly power.

It was probably just as well for the papal temper that, furious at the fall of 'his' city to Vittorio Emmanuele and his 'band of brigands', he had locked himself inside his basilica of St John Lateran. The new secular authorities held a plebiscite on 2 October 1870, and, of those who voted, only a little over one per cent were in favour of being ruled by him rather than King Vittorio Emmanuele; in Rome itself, the figure was just over 0.1 percent.

A dramatic contemporary image of the fall of Rome to the troops of Vittorio Emmanuele: *The Breach of Porta Pia* by Michele Cammarano (1849-1920)

The Pope had commanded all Catholics to have nothing to do with politics, but, under a franchise wider than any seen again in Italy for nearly half a century, not all the faithful or even all priests obeyed him: some clearly voted against him. There was clearly little sentimental attachment to autocratic Papal rule, even in towns like Montecompatri, which had a long direct association with the Papacy.

Pius would have been even more annoyed had he attended sessions of the new governing assembly of Rome, the *Giunta di Roma*, where the 'Law of Guarantees', detailing the Pope's status in the new Italian state, was being debated. He would hardly have enjoyed hearing one supposedly moderate member of the *Giunta*, Ruggero Bonghi, end a speech with the words: 'If you are Catholics, then thank Heaven that the [Pope's] temporal rule is at an end; the greatest and most shameful sore on the body of the Catholic church in the whole world has been healed.'[37]

At the 1871 census Rome, with a population of under a quarter of a million, was by no means the largest city in Italy; that honour was held by Naples (about 450,000). Milan, at some 262,000, was also larger. At this date London had about 3,250,000 inhabitants, Paris about 1,850,000 and New York a little under one-and-a half million.[36]

The Pontifical response to such secular temerity was rapid. In his encyclical *Respicientes* of 1 November he denounced 'the Italian occupation of the territories of the Holy See' as 'unjust, violent, null and void', and excommunicated all concerned, from monarch to common soldier. Refusing to hand over the keys of the Quirinal Palace (his temporal seat), he 'fulminated against the King as a new Attila'[38] and sulked, referring to himself as 'the prisoner of the Vatican'. Furious he remained, and impotent.

Amidst this volatile situation, Moreschi was enrolled at the choir-school run by the Fratelli delle Scuole Cristiani at the church of San Salvatore in Lauro, situated in the baroque heart of Rome to the north-west of Piazza Navona. This was hardly a safe haven, since, like many other prestigious Roman institutions, it was a papal foundation, dating from the late 18th century. (It actually survived as a training ground for papal singers until 1904.)[39] Moreover, this *schola cantorum* had, in 1868, become specifically a *schola puerorum* or school for training boy musicians, at the express wish of Pius IX himself. This had come about as a direct result of a memorable performance in St Peter's Basilica of the motet *Tu es Petrus*, written and directed by Domenico Mustafà, (the most famous soprano castrato of his day, who had been a member of the Sistine Choir since 1848) in which some 300

In einem Neste des St. Peter ist ein Ei gelegt worden, das ausgebrütet die Tauben aus aller Welt zusammengelockt werden.

A contemporary German cartoon mocks Pope Pius IX's self-incarceration

boys, recruited from churches throughout Rome, sang alongside the castrati and other professional voices of the papal choirs. At this time the received wisdom in Italy and many other countries was still that boys could not be trained to high standards of singing - what an erroneous contrast to the Anglican tradition! It is a great irony that Mustafà should in this sense have been responsible for sowing the seeds of destruction of his own voice-type, since the improved standard of boys' singing did eventually make them viable choral substitutes for the castrati.

The school was divided into senior and junior classes, each of three sections streamed for ability, with yearly examinations for promotion to the next division. Vocal tuition at the school was free (piano and violin were available at a small extra cost), and the pupils were even paid a small stipend for their public perform-ances, called *accademie* and *saggi*. The former were basically public concerts held on school premises, the latter more like end-of-term performance 'essays' (the word's literal meaning). The opera-based repertoire for both was a far cry from the boys' most important vocal function beyond the school walls, namely singing at the office of Tenebrae in St Peter's Basilica during Holy Week.

Thirteen years old when he arrived in Rome, Moreschi was, as far as is known, the only castrato of school age (the contralto, and later *soprano acuto* at the Sistine Chapel, Domenico Salvatori was already 16), and his uniquely uncomfortable situation was no doubt brought home to him by the taunts of his schoolfellows. As a country boy in the big city, he would have felt lonely in any case, but it was probably during these years of schooling that he first began to realise just how alone he would be for the rest of his life. Unlike the other boys, he would not undergo, or enjoy, puberty.

The outward effects of castration on his adolescent body were considerable. Unlike his contemporaries, there would have been no opportunity for him to encourage his first beard or moustache. His skin would have remained 'baby soft', with no masculine coarsening of its texture. On the other hand, he would have had no acne, nor suffered a voice cracking and breaking beyond his control. Spared embarrassment in these respects at least, he undoubtedly suffered it in many other ways. Roman schoolboys of the time would have been as fascinated by sex as adolescents always are, but Alessandro would probably have found any 'dirty talk' bewildering, even irrelevant. The supposed sexual abilities of earlier castrati had long been the subject of gossip and scandal, so he probably was the butt of much related ribaldry. However, it would seem that, for most castrati, the libido acted at a very reduced level, and this would have been especially noticeable during the adolescent period of raging hormones. The production of male sex hormones is not entirely dependent on the testes ('weak' androgens are also produced in the suprarenal glands, for example), but the weak hormones present in Alessandro's teenage body could only have had a small effect, such as perhaps causing his penis to enlarge somewhat from its infantile state in the normal course of bodily growth. One consequence of a lack of testosterone is a tendency to put on extra body fat, particularly on the chest and buttocks, though in Moreschi's case, this seems not to happened until after his teens. He was also lucky not to suffer from another disfigurement for which castrati were often mocked: another function of testosterone is to cause the epiphyses (joint-ends) in the skeleton to harden, and without it, a castrato's arms and legs would often keep growing to a grotesque extent. Many 18th-century cartoons of operatic castrati bear witness to this.

Moreschi in his teens

Psychologically, castration can also, not surprisingly, have a deleterious effect on self-esteem (which of course can be a problem in any teenager's life), and any possible worries about sexual identity may have been complicated in Alessandro's case by an awareness, however little understood or expressed, of the uniqueness of his physical state. Castration itself does not affect sexuality, and there is no evidence that Moreschi was homosexual. His no doubt conventional Catholic upbringing would have made expression or discussion of such worries and feelings difficult, if not impossible. Nonetheless, however problematic his adolescent inner life may have been, the emotional outlet of musical performance, which now played a dominant role in his life, may well have been a saving grace. Here was something at least in which his lack had a positive aspect.

The teaching he received in the *schola cantorum* was certainly of a high standard. Under the headmastership of Brother Vincenzo Torre, the practical training of the pupils at San Lauro was in the hands of the choirmasters of Rome's three patriarchal basilicas,[40] one of whom, Gaetano Capocci, master of music at the Pope's own cathedral of St John Lateran, became Moreschi's teacher.

Capocci was an enormously important influence on his young pupil. Born in Rome in 1811, he was involved with the church music of the city for the whole of his working life. His first organ teacher was Pascoli, then organist of St Peter's, and Capocci's own first post was as organist, from 1830 to 1839, of Santa Maria in Valicella, (also, incidentally, the church in which the burial vault of the papal singers had long been situated).[41] His appointments as President of the Organists of the Accademia di Santa Cecilia in 1848, at a time when it was becoming a conservatoire in the modern sense, and as Master of the Music at the Lateran in 1855, had placed him at the very centre of Roman musical life.

Beginning in the 1850s, he had also acquired a reputation as an important composer of sacred music in what was termed the 'neo-theatrical' style, close in manner, if not necessarily in inspiration, to the operas of Bellini, Donizetti, and Giuseppe

A conservatoire was originally a charitable institution for the education of orphans, though an element of specialisation in music had been present from an early date. The oldest of these were the Venetian *ospedali*, of which the first, the Ospedale dei Mendicanti, was founded in 1262. The oldest existing conservatoire in today's sense of 'a public place of instruction in any special branch, esp. music and the arts', to quote Webster, is the Kungliga Musikhögskolan in Stockholm, founded in 1771.

Verdi, the greatest Italian composer alive at that time. In addition, during his early career, Capocci had become a favourite in ecclesiastical circles for his writing of *rifacimenti*, re-workings of operas to religious texts. Since Pope Benedict XIV's *De dioecesana synodo* (see p 18) all clerics and monastics had been forbidden to attend the theatre on moral grounds, so such re-workings were their only means of keeping up with the latest operatic trends. Capocci's own *rifacimenti* included a version of Rossini's *Semiramide*, probably featuring Mustafà, in his singing prime during the 1860s, in the title-role.[42] It is hard to resist the idea that these occasions, which usually took place after dark, had a distinct element of the camp about them: the vision of the candle-lit Chiesa Nuova, where castrati had first sung in Rome nearly 300 years earlier, (and apparently a great favourite for these crepuscular happenings) filled with clerics in rustling purple and black listening entranced to an artificially-preserved male voice as it trilled its way through a Rossini cabaletta in the character of the Queen of Babylon must truly have been something extraordinary. After dark, no respectable woman could be present: all-male cabaret has a long history.

Though in the Rome of 1871 such decadent carryings-on were, at least officially, as extinct as the Pope's temporal rule, it was precisely such operatic music, in the form of solos, duets and the like, that featured in the public performances given by the boys of San Salvatore in Lauro. These gave Alessandro an enduring taste for such repertoire, and would also have afforded him regular sips of power: that special and intoxicating relationship between audience and performer. Priests and singers from the Vatican must have known (not least from Rosati) of the unique presence of Moreschi at the school, while Mustafà, already becoming as well known as a composer and director as he had been as a singer, would have already been keeping an eye on him as a possible successor. Himself a traditionalist to his fingertips, Mustafà had probably always hoped that the school, as a gathering place for gifted boy singers, would reveal those of particular talent who were ripe for the knife.

Alessandro clearly made rapid progress, since, as early as July 1873, Capocci appointed him to the post of *primo soprano* at St John Lateran, where he soon began to acquire a following. He was only 15 years old, like so many castrati of earlier times taking on an important public singing role at a very tender age. He was lucky enough to avoid a vocal problem, which beset many young castrati: a period of vocal uncertainty during teenage years in parallel with the breaking voice of a whole adolescent. Teenage castrato huskiness is thought to have been caused by proto-androgens produced in the male body in the years leading up to puberty, which would still have been secreted if castration was carried out late. Nowadays these hormones often cause a boy soprano's voice, especially a long-lasting one, to acquire increased strength and tonal edge in the few months before it breaks. This is further evidence that Moreschi was castrated well before he came to Rome.

A useful source for reports of Moreschi's youthful performances is found in the memoirs of Anna Lillie de Hegemann-Lindencrone (1844-1928), the American wife of the Danish ambassador to Italy in the 1880s, and herself a talented singer. From Rome she wrote to one of her aunts during Holy Week 1881: 'The churches are open all day. St Peter's, Laterano, Santa Maria Maggiore each has one of the famous sopranos . . . Good Friday is the great day at St Peter's. The church is so crowded that one can hardly get a place to stand . . . My servant generally carries a camp-stool and rug, and I sit entranced, listening in the deepening twilight to the heavenly strains of Palestrina, Pergolese [*sic*] and Marcello. Sometimes the soloists sing Gounod's 'Ava [*sic*] Maria' and Rossini's 'Stabat Mater', and, fortunately, drown the squeaky tones of the old organ. A choir of men and boys accompanies them in 'The Inflammatus' [*sic*], where the high notes of M[oreschi]'s tearful voice are almost supernatural.

People swarm to the Laterano on Saturday to hear the Vespers, which are especially fine.'[43]

Participation in paid public concerts, referred to by the authorities as 'venal academies', was officially forbidden by the Bull *Cum Retinendi* of Clement XIII, promulgated in 1762, but Papal singers were permitted to sing at private gatherings, and Moreschi soon became a member of a select group of performers that Capocci employed at such soirées. Here the fashionable salon and operatic music of the day was *de rigueur*, and Mrs de Hegemann-Lindencrone an avid witness to the proceedings: 'Mrs Charles Bristed of New York, a recent convert to the Church of Rome, receives on Saturday evening . . . The Pope's singers

Mrs de Hegemann-Lindencrone (née Greenough) had shown such precocious vocal talent that, at the age of 15, she went with her mother to Paris to study with the world-famous Manuel García. There she married Charles Moulton, the son of a wealthy American banker, and soon her beauty and singing ability made her the talk of Parisian society. As well as her memoirs, she wrote a fascinating account of her early years and of life in Paris at the time of Napoleon III, entitled *In the Courts of Memory*. At the fall of the French Empire she returned to America, and after Moulton's death married Johan Henrik de Hegemann-Lindencrone, at that time Danish Minister to the USA.

are the great attraction . . . for her salon is the only place outside of the churches where one can hear them. The famous Moresca [sic], who sings at the Laterano, is a full-faced soprano of some forty winters.[44] He has a tear in each note and a sigh in each breath. He sang the jewel song [*sic*] in [Gounod's] 'Faust', which seemed horribly out of place. Especially when he asks (in the hand-glass) if he is really Marguerita, one feels tempted to answer 'Macchè' [not in the least] for him.'[45]

Marguerite's 'Jewel Song' requires a flexible coloratura technique over a two-octave range, and would have been an ideal musical showpiece for the young singer, for all the oddness of the vocal transvestism. Mrs Grace Bristed was the widow of the writer Charles Astor Bristed (1820-1874), of the fabulously wealthy New York Astor family. Their son, also called Charles (1868-1936), became a chamberlain to Popes Leo XIII, Pius X and Benedict XV. There is likely to have been a long-standing link between this prominent Catholic convert and circles close to the Vatican hierarchy, which would have enabled her to obtain the services of the Pope's own singers. Her Catholicism would also have made her suitable in papal eyes for the employing of papal singers: by contrast, the Sistine records in March 1857, for example, recorded the punishment of Rosati, Moreschi's first teacher, and Mustafà (in spite of his fame), for having taken part in an *accademia* 'in the house of a protestant'.[46] Mrs Bristed's artistic taste, Catholic faith and foreign status also helped her to accomplish 'what has hitherto been considered impossible – that is the bringing together of the "blacks" (the ultra-Catholic party, adhering to the Vatican) and the "whites", the party adhering to the Quirinal. These two parties meet in her salon as if they were of the same colour . . .'.[47] Such unofficial propinquity preceded official rapprochement between church and state by over 40 years.

It is noteworthy in the adjacent picture that Moreschi and his soprano colleague Cesari are both dressed in a conspicuously elegant way, though Salvatori looks distinctly lugubrious (he also has huge hands, a common feature of castrati). There is further evidence of Alessandro's vanity: 'Moreschi's behaviour was often capricious enough to make him forget a proper professional bearing, as on the occasion after a concert when he paraded himself among the crowd like a peacock, with a long, white scarf, to be congratulated . . .'.[48] On the other hand, he certainly had good reason to be pleased with himself, and was not averse to using the acclaim

1ª Alasandro Moreschi. Soprano
2ª Antonio Cotogni. Baritono
3ª Giovanni Cesari . Soprano (acuto)
4ª M.ᵉ Filippo Mattoni Contralto

Moreschi and 'concert party' colleagues (seated left to right: Moreschi, Antonio Cotogni, Giovanni Cesari; standing left to right (probably) Giovanni Capocci, Filippo Mattoni, (certainly) Domenico Salvatori). As Mrs de Hegemann-Lindencrone stated in her account of Mrs Bristed's salon concerts 'Maroni [sic] is the man who always directs the Pope's singers'; Cotogni, was a famous baritone, who had a major international career from 1860 until his retirement in 1898. Is 'Giovanni' Capocci a slip of the pen? Nothing would have been more natural than for Maestro Gaetano Capocci to have sung at such soirées as well. None of the singers is in orders, since all wear 'normal' street dress of some kind — it is likely that actual participation in salon concerts by priests was frowned upon.

he received and the demand for his services to his own advantage, perhaps particularly where he could extract extra financial reward: 'It happened once in the Confraternity of Santa Maria dell' Orto in Trastevere, for the feast of 8 September, that the hour of pontifical mass had to be moved from 11 o'clock to midday because Moreschi was engaged elsewhere before that time. So for once at least the celebrant bishop had to subordinate himself to the need of the singer.'[49] This service for the Feast of the Nativity of the Blessed Virgin Mary would have been a confraternity celebration conducted for a lay religious organisation in a working-class parish. They had probably hired Moreschi as a guest soloist on what would have been for him a very busy day, Our Lady being the patron of many Roman churches. Some of his other venues that day were no doubt considerably more *signorile* (a richly meaningful word in Italian with special overtones of 'better class') and so this parish had to wait for him. Moreschi was himself of humble origin and was certainly in many ways a social outcast, so no doubt gloried in the prominence he had achieved as a member of the Papal Chapel (still technically a 'royal' institution) and in the salons of Roman high society, however ambivalent the attitudes of some members of his audiences might have been.

There were certainly some in the Roman hierarchy who thought Moreschi went too far. Maestro Meluzzi, Master of Music at the Cappella Giulia, complained to his superior, the Prefect of Music at St Peter's, that ' . . . he sang on Wednesday in the Ven[erabile] Chiesa del Sudario in splendid vocal condition; the next day, Thursday, he could not make himself available in San Pietro for the solennità della Cattedra [the Feast of St Peter's Chair] on account of a rather sudden vocal decline; today, in most splendid vocal state, he was able to perform a funeral mass at the Chiesa di San Carlo in Corso. Monsignor de Nekere has described this perfectly. Excuse me for the trouble I put you to with this disagreeable tale. It does not seem proper to me that the Vatican

Chapter should be dictated to by the whim of a hermaphrodite' (letter dated Friday 19 January 1883).[50]

This is a deliciously sour example of Vatican tale-bearing and bitchiness, justified by sticking to the letter of the law. Meluzzi was ostensibly Capocci's equal (or even superior, considering the status of St Peter's Basilica), but probably had a lower public profile. Here he seems to be using bit of tittle-tattle from a self-righteous cleric to try to damage the reputation of a favourite singer of a rival conductor. In literal terms, he was well within his rights, since Moreschi certainly had infringed one of the *Ordini* ('Regulations') of the Cappella Giulia, that relating to 'absence without proper cause'. However, all this took place just two months before Moreschi's appointment to the Sistine and so motives of jealousy cannot be discounted. Alessandro was, of course, trying to have his cake and eat it, by taking on two paid outside jobs while avoiding the responsibility of an appearance covered by his salary, and Meluzzi knew that the singer's infringement, if discovered, would lead to loss of pay. As his pejorative use of the term 'hermaphrodite' shows, he also hypocritically regarded Moreschi as beyond the pale simply for being a castrato, for all that he employed him and his like in his choir. The letter shows in addition that singers at one papal basilica were already, by this date, appearing at others.

Meanwhile, Moreschi's teacher Capocci seems to have had his pupil's career prospects very much in mind, and was determined to show his *protégé* off to public advantage. During Lent 1883, at his own church of St John Lateran, he arranged a performance of Beethoven's oratorio *Christus am Ölberge* ('Christ on the Mount of Olives') as a vehicle for Alessandro's talents. The work, in which the 25-year old castrato sang the important and vocally demanding role of the Seraph, was performed in an Italian version (*Cristo all' Uliveto*) made by an Austrian military official and musicologist, Franz Sales Kandler (1792-1831), and published by Ricordi of

Milan as long ago as 1825.[51] This was apparently the piece's first complete performance in Italy, and brought Moreschi both great public acclaim and also the sobriquet 'L'Angelo di Roma' ('The Angel of Rome'), by which he was ever afterwards known. The Seraph's part is written for high soprano, with optional notes up to e''' (just a semitone below the highest note written for the Queen of the Night in Mozart's *Die Zauberflöte*) and demands considerable agility in its many florid passages and wide leaps. Although the actual musical style is very different, such ornate coloratura is a close parallel to the astounding technical demands made on castrati of earlier generations, for whom flexibility of voice had been a *sine qua non*. More importantly for the direction of Moreschi's future career his performance was so successful that 'he was invited to apply for admission to the Sistine Chapel',[52] and thus he obtained the soprano post in the Choir which had fallen vacant during Advent 1882, on the retirement of the castrato Evangelista Bocchini (1827-1888).

The Cappella Musicale Pontificia

Although he had been a member of the Cappella Lateranense
for ten years, becoming a member of the *Cappella Musicale
Pontificia* (the Sistine Chapel Choir's official designation) must
have been something of a culture shock for Alessandro. The
basilica of St John Lateran was, and is, a huge, public cathedral,
whereas the Sistine is comparatively small, and the private
chapel of the Pope himself: an almost secret, and certainly
secretive organisation, the defensiveness of which can only
have been heightened by the turmoils it had witnessed in
Europe during the previous hundred years. In this it was no
more than a microcosm of the Papacy as a whole, an organisation whose complex hierarchy of cardinals, monsignors,
chamberlains, major-domos and the like (not to mention Swiss
Guards) would now enswathe Moreschi for the remainder of
his active life.

For all that the Vatican had chosen to ignore recent political
upheavals as much as was possible, these did eventually have an
effect on the Pope and all in his employ, far beyond the loss of
papal temporal power. This in itself was in marked contrast to
the Sistine Chapel's previous long and largely undisturbed history.
The original papal *schola cantorum* ('school of singers') dated
from the fourth century, but it was after the 'Babylonian
captivity' of the popes in Avignon (1309-1377) that it came to
be fixed, in that thereafter it always performed in the Pope's
church or chapel. The title Sistine derives from Pope Sixtus IV

The Sistine Chapel (photographed prior to the restoration
of Michelangelo's frescoes)

(reigned 1471-1484) who had had built the chapel that now bears his name. The members of the choir were officially known as the *cappellani cantori pontifici* (literally pontificial singing chaplains, reflecting their official status as clerics in minor orders). The term 'Cappella Sistina' is a 19th-century invention: the diaries of the German composer Otto Nicolai, who became organist to the Prussian Embassy in Rome in 1833, are an early source for the term.

The make-up of the choir was also first fixed during the 15th century. After 1441, there is no mention in the choir records of boys' voices being used, and in a Bull of November 1483, Sixtus ordained that the choir should have 24 members, six of each voice. The sopranos were certainly falsettists at this date, but whether the altos were that, or were rather high tenors, remains controversial. Musicological arguments have raged for years over the who, what, where and why of falsettists, counter-tenors and *hautes-contres* (a French type of high tenor). Recent scholarly research tends to exclude falsettist counter-tenors (like Alfred Deller and his many successors) from much of the repertoire in which 'counter-tenors' have become familiar in recent years, though the arguments used are not wholly convincing. The human larynx is capable of a flexibility many scholars might envy: one member of the Sistine Chapel Choir in the 19th century, Alessandro Chiari (1824-1878), had been admitted to Rome's Accademia di Santa Cecilia as a *contralto cantante* in 1841, but four years later transferred to the *classe dei bassi*. His Sistine colleague Gabrielli referred to him as a 'fine tenor'.[53] It does seem, though that most contraltos in the Sistine Choir were, from at least 1700 to the mid-19th century, tenors with a high falsetto-like extension (castrato contraltos, frequently encountered elsewhere, were hardly ever employed there). Not long after the innovations of Donzelli and Duprez there were complaints about the changes in the voice-quality and production of those applying for posts: '. . . each candidate must present a voice of the true character that we are looking for . . . for the performance of modern music tenor and bass voices especially call for another character than that suitable for service in the Sistine Chapel.'[54] This would not least have been because the more robust modern way of singing would have conflicted with the old-style technique of the remaining castrati. As far as the tenors themselves were concerned, use of the new heavier registration would usually have prevented them from keeping the light, high, falsetto-like timbre of earlier times. They would hardly have worried a great deal about that, since the former manner of singing had rapidly fallen out of fashion. (Most modern counter-tenors generally use a different balance of vocal registration, using falsetto for most of their range, with perhaps a few notes of more-or-less well-blended ordinary voice in the lower regions. It should be remembered that all adult males are physiologically capable of producing sounds in the falsetto register.)

To return to Sistine history: in 1512, Pope Julius II founded the Cappella Giulia at St Peter's as something like a choir school for the Sistine, while Leo X (1513-1521) established that the master of the choir should henceforward be in the first instance a musician, irrespective of his clerical rank. Paul III's *Constitutiones Cappellae Pontificiae* of 1545 established the choir's constitution for the next three centuries and more, including rules for the election of new members, who were first proposed by the choir-master and then vetted by the existing members (*maior et senior pars*). Without specific permission, the members of the Sistine were forbidden to sing other than in the Pope's service. These regulations, and many others, remained essentially unaltered until 1891, and oblivious to the social, religious and economic upheavals that might beset the world outside, the yearly round of divine worship continued largely unaltered.

It was the cataclysm of the Napoleonic Wars that at last marked a point of definitive change for the Cappella Sistina, in a manner which was to have a direct effect on Moreschi's life, though this is only obvious with the benefit of hindsight. At the time, for all that the French invaded Italy in 1798 and conquered Rome (to the extent indeed of kidnapping Pope Pius VII), the maelstrom that was Napoleon's Europe may have seemed to have as little influence inside the Vatican as any other secular event. The political and social climate of much of Europe after the Congresses of Vienna (1814 and 1815) was deeply conservative, and the Catholic Church was for a long while determined to behave as if the little Corsican, and all the revolutionary and republican currents of thought that swirled about him, had never existed.

The French occupation did, however, have obvious and immediate effects. Between the deposition of the Pope on 10 June 1809 and his first return on 24 May 1814 the papal chapels were suppressed. The papal singers refused to sing a *Te Deum* for Napoleon's coronation (on 30 November 1809), and were thereafter subjected to various forms of intimidation in order to procure their services. The French also attempted to amalgamate the Cappella Sistina and Cappella Giulia into one Imperial Chapel, but most members of both choirs again refused to collaborate, preferring loss of income to disloyalty to their spiritual and temporal sovereign. The papal chapels remained silent for five years, the Sistine Diaries blank.

Even after the Pope's definitive second restoration of 7 June 1815 (there had been the minor hiccough of Napoleon's unexpected return from Elba), the outlook for the members of the Cappella Sistina was none too good, not least in that their pleas to Pius VII for payment of the salaries they had lost during five years of loyal silence fell on deaf ears. On the other hand, they were lucky in the person of their Director, Giuseppe Baini (1775-

1844), admitted to the choir as a bass singer in 1795 and its *de facto* conductor from about 1817. He was the most important figure in the Chapel's music for the next quarter-century, being eventually named *Direttore perpetuo* in 1841.

Baini's determination to uphold and revitalise the choir's traditions was much appreciated by the Cappella. The Sistine Diary for 1817 stated 'never can the tireless care that our most worthy *maestro* takes for the good of us all and in all respects be sufficiently praised . . .'.[55] His wish to see high performance standards was not always popular: in 1838 rehearsals were made obligatory, replacing the traditional requirement of merely attending the Chapel's daily sung office. This move led to absenteeism and boycotts. (Conflicts over discipline continued sporadically throughout the 19th century.) Perhaps aware of a change in the social climate Baini also made an early attempt to have boys trained for the Sistine Choir without being castrated, but in the conservative post-Restoration Vatican, this idea was soon dropped. By 1819, the situation was becoming serious: 'The present and also future impossibility of finding sopranos for the service of our chapel threatened a crisis for the College. Therefore the conductor joined with the gentlemen sopranos in supplicating the Holy Father to the effect that he might allow them to search throughout Italy for four castrated boys, to be admitted into the venerable Pia Casa degl' Orfani, such that they might be educated in piety and instructed in music . . . '.[56] On this occasion, three suitable boys were found, and admitted as requested, their fees being paid from choir funds. Recruitment of castrati remained a problem throughout the century, while the attractions of the secular theatre in particular made finding other voices increasingly difficult. Even those already members of the Sistine sometimes jumped ship: in 1817, one Francesco Reali had jumped as far as Rio de Janeiro. In an attempt at least to keep up the appearance of numbers, many of the papal singers of the 19th century were granted an extension to their contract (and more pay) in a *secondo servizio* ('second service'), and some even a third. It thus became not unusual to see singers well into their seventies singing in the Sistine Choir. In 1836, Pope Gregory XVI passed a decree temporarily forbidding the acceptance of laymen, except as sopranos. This was ostensibly in order to prevent the proportion of non-clerical singers from rising above one third and thus damaging the Chapel's identity as an 'ecclesiastical college', but was really something of a panic measure: after the 1819 intake, three more castrati were admitted between 1822 and 1831, but then none at all until 1848, when the twenty-year-old Domenico Mustafà arrived. He was to prove a standard bearer for Sistine traditions for a further half century.

In the long run, this was to prove most fortunate, since Baini's death in 1844 had marked the beginning of a period of real decline for the Sistine chapel Choir. He had been the first choir master to be named *Direttore perpetuo*, and, since that title was not sanctified by long tradition, he was not replaced. The hierarchical nature of the choir's organisation reasserted itself, and for well over 30 years its performances were led, as the same tradition demanded, by the senior bass singer, known as the *basso del finestrino*, (presumably from where he stood, nearest to a window). The dangers of using seniority as a criterion for leadership were soon obvious: the first such director, Padre Felice da Cantalice, was dismissed for his 'scant ability', and his successors seem to have been men of no great skill either.

This was indeed a sorry state of affairs, but one possible source of better things was to come in the election of a new pontiff. On 16 June 1846, the white smoke of the Conclave and the well-worn phrase *habemus papam* ('we have a pope') signalled the election of Giovanni Maria Mastai-Ferretti, Bishop of Imola, who took the name Pius IX. In 1831, while Archbishop of Spoleto, he had interceded with the Austrian army on behalf of 4,000 Italian revolutionaries who were threatening the city, obtaining their pardon: such actions had gained him the reputation of something of a liberal. In contrast to his conservative predecessor Gregory XVI, Pius, 'a Pope of singular goodness and singular charm', had been seen at the beginning of his pontificate as a reforming spirit who understood ' . . . the necessity of carrying out reforms and righting wrongs . . . Men became convinced that a Pope had arisen who was destined to set the seal on the unification of Italy, to reconcile and satisfy unitarian and anti-Austrian aspirations, and at the same time to manifest his devotion to the religion of his forebears and to the ideal of representative government. The Pope was a prisoner of the enthusiasms he had aroused.'[57]

A prisoner indeed: though himself aware of the recent deterioration of standards at the Sistine Chapel and desirous of making amends, he was overtaken by larger events. The years 1848 and 1849 saw revolutionary risings against authority in (amongst other cities) Berlin, Vienna, Naples, Venice, Milan, Prague and Budapest. A republic was proclaimed in Rome, and the Pope was forced into temporary exile. During his 18 months' sojourn in Gaëta, Pius's mind, perhaps not surprisingly, turned completely away from any paths of change, and for the remaining 28 years of his pontificate the Papacy was a bulwark of conservatism. Under the watchful eye of Giacomo Cardinal Antonelli, the Papal Secretary of State and real power behind the throne, the Vatican establishment continued much as before. The Sistine Chapel's routine was undisturbed, though there were continuing worries about the lack of personnel, and about the financial situation of both the organisation as a whole and its members. In the larger world, Papal detestation of change was most famously demonstrated by the encyclical *Quanta Cura* of 8 December 1864, in which the Pius condemned all 'errors of liberalism' and sought to enforce church control of such things as education and the

Pope Pius IX: a portrait painted at his accession by Pietro Chatelain

sacrament of marriage. All to no avail: the first attacks of Vittorio Emmanuele's army came at the end of October 1867, and on 8 November the Sistine Chapel Choir sang a requiem mass for soldiers fallen in the Papal service. For the next couple of years those singers who lived outside Rome often found themselves prevented from getting to their work by the presence of the King's forces.

The end was not long in coming: in 1870, after over twenty years of the *Risorgimento*, the Papal States finally succumbed. Having survived over a thousand years of squabbling between prelates and princes, Italy was at last a unified state, with Rome its new, secular capital.

As one noted authority has put it 'the [Papal] State expired under the Pontificate of one of the most sentimental and impulsive Popes ever possessed by the Church',[58] and Pius certainly now showed some of this side of his nature with regard to his musical establishment, one of the few organisations with a public profile beyond the Vatican over which he still retained absolute power. He suspended sixty-eight of the Sistine Chapel's musical obligations, retaining only the Holy Week and Easter celebrations as a regular event, and closing everything to the public for the remainder of his pontificate. This may have been pique on his part, but as far as the choir was concerned there were serious knock-on effects: 'no disciplinary orders were issued, no voice-searches undertaken . . . a general and clear abrogation of decrees, interest and tradition, accumulated little by little. A real disaster. Seven years were enough to destroy the work of centuries.'[59]

The disastrous nature of the 1870 'shut-down' was particularly regrettable in that the Sistine Chapel Choir had at least physically survived the upheavals of [1848 to 1849] largely intact, though three singers had been expelled for 'perhaps having been mixed up . . . in the seditious and anarchic republican government.'[60] The young Mustafà had himself been somewhat 'mixed up' in such matters, having performed at least twice at events in St Peter's Basilica attended by members of the new secular authority. He was, however, lucky enough to be treated with greater indulgence (perhaps he was just too good a singer to lose), and rapidly became known as the finest castrato of his day. His singing even came to the notice of Richard Wagner, who is said to have originally wanted him to take the role of the magician Klingsor in his opera *Parsifal* (1882). That nothing came of this may be at least partly laid to the fact that by this date Mustafà's voice may have already been past its best: he was 54 years old, and had qualified for his choir pension four years previously.

That year, 1878, also saw the end of Pius IX's pontificate, which, at almost 32 years, was the longest in history (perhaps excepting that of St Peter himself). The new pontiff, Leo XIII, took great delight in listening to 'his' choir, but was also concerned to tighten the observance of the choir's regulations and generally to reinvigorate the whole organisation.

Mustafà had been *Direttore dei Concertisti* ('Director of Soloists')[61] to the choir since 1861. He was the only member of the Sistine establishment to hold such a long-term musical directorship, and this was helping him to become the Chapel's dominant musical personality, both as composer and conductor. Like the Pope he was a man bent on reviving the choir's fortunes, the achievement of which would hardly do his reputation any harm. Not afraid of pushing for Papal attention, he had written several works for the special audiences and private concerts held for Pius IX and continued in the same vein for Leo, notably directing his own music, and some by Baini, in a special *accademia poliglotta* ('multilingual private concert') given for the Pope 'to console him in his prison', as reported in the Vatican newspaper *L'Osservatore Romano* for 20 April 1880.

There was clearly a meeting of minds, or at least objectives,

Pope Leo was also concerned to preserve the fabric of the Sistine chapel as a building, installing a heating system so that the famous frescoes by Michelangelo would not suffer too much from temperature extremes. No doubt the members of the choir were grateful for this too, since Andrea Bregno's beautiful *Cantoria* (choir-loft) looks decidedly draughty!

here. Mustafà was the obvious person to lead the revival of the choir's more public activities, which Pope Leo desired. However, the Supreme Pontiff's wishes notwithstanding, this was not achieved with total ease. Internal tensions bedevilled the Sistine's close-knit community, largely due to jealousy of Mustafà, whom at least a few choir-members thought overly power-hungry. Vincenzo Tuzzi, the titular 'Director of the Choir' (as senior bass he was the latest in the line of 'basses of the window' in succession to Baini), was in poor health, and so could be dealt with without too much difficulty; but the senior contralto and composer Innocenzo Pasquali was another matter altogether, and potentially a serious threat to Mustafà's position.

The basis of the rivalry between the two men lay in a fundamental disagreement in attitudes to the composition of sacred music. Pasquali was something of a standard-bearer for the deliberately archaising *stile prenestino* ('Palestrina style') of composition, adhering strictly to perceived compositional rules which were by this time some 300 years old. This tendency seems to have told against him with others, the Pope included. Mustafà was more pragmatic and more inclined to compose in a mixed style which incorporated melodic and harmonic procedures derived from those of contemporary opera.

The trigger for this particular conflict was, however, not really musical at all: on 10 February 1881, the Sistine Diary recorded that Pasquali had prevented Mustafà from attending the voice-trials for two prospective new members of the choir, and also publicly challenged the validity of Mustafà's position as 'Director of Soloists'. (One of the last acts of Pope Pius IX had been to reinforce Mustafà's position by the addition of the adjective *perpetuo* to the title: this is well documented.)[62] It is also true that to give Mustafà, a soprano, Tuzzi's title would have been to break with tradition, and Pasquali lost no time in pointing this out, (though this would also have been the case had he been appointed).

Mustafà felt unjustifiably assailed and, not for the first time, went off in a huff, declaring that 'the College entrusted me with the beat, and I am sending it back to them'.[63] Beat is 'battuta' in Italian, but this word can also mean 'wisecrack', so figuratively he was also saying something like 'My colleagues think they can make a joke at my expense; I send it back to them with interest'. Pasquali received little support from the other members of the choir, who rapidly realised that Mustafà was too good a director to cast off in this fashion, and begged him to return. After a few weeks of further toing and froing, and mollified by Pope Leo's granting him the title of *Direttore generale in perpetuo*, Mustafà was prevailed upon to take up his new duties. One wonders whether his whole flounce was not an elaborate bluff, designed to flush out Pasquali's rivalry, and which he knew would not be called.

For years acknowledged as a singer of the highest calibre, Mustafà now occupied a unique position in Rome's musical life. In the secular field he was already 'Musical President' of the renowned *Società Musicale*

A photograph of Domenico Mustafà c 1850

Romana, with whom his notable conducting appearances included the Italian premiere of Handel's *Messiah* in 1876. His Perpetual Directorship of the Sistine Chapel Choir was quite simply a position of unmatchable prestige: a remarkable achievement for a man of poor peasant stock, and a member of a much-abused 'voice minority'. The air of the Sistine may have cleared, and Pasquali been made to eat humble pie, but the unique combination of Italian character and performer's ego under strict regulation and church protocol would always make for a potentially stormy working atmosphere. The sudden appearance of a new star soloist in March 1883 would have done little to calm any troubles of Mustafà's early directorial years, however much he now received official support at the highest level.

Moreschi's early years
at the Sistine Chapel 1883-1891

'To His Holiness Pope Leo XIII
Most Holy Father,

Alessandro Moreschi, aged twenty-five, native of Monte
Compatri, prostrates himself to kiss your holy foot, and humbly
declares that, having for several years found himself a singer in
the arch-basilica of the Lateran in the post of First Soprano,
and, now desiring to apply for the same in the Sistine Chapel,
states that he does not possess that single requisite demanded by
the Regulations for those applying in the capacity of soprano in
the said chapel.

The declarer warmly begs Your Holiness to deign to heal
the said defect.

Who, etc.
Alessandro Moreschi'

The original Italian of Moreschi's official letter of application
to the Pope is every bit as convoluted and recondite as its translation,
and may itself be seen as symptomatic of the still unchanging
nature of Vatican protocol at this time. There is much irony in the
phrase 'he does not possess that single requisite', since, being
without the 'requisites of virility', he did retain the precious requisite
of his soprano voice. The 'requisite' that he actually needed was
Papal sanction, and this he received, being duly elected to his

singing post *per rescritto* ('by rescript', a Papal rescript being an official Papal reply to an individual petition), dated 22 March 1883. Officially castrati were still forbidden clerical status, but members of the Sistine Choir were required to take at least 'minor orders'.

At the time of Moreschi's arrival there were six other castrati in the choir: Gustavo Pesci (1833-1913, admitted 1864), Giuseppe Ritarossi (1841-1902, admitted 1864), Giosafat Vissani (1841-?1904/16, admitted 1866), Giovanni Cesari (1843-1904, admitted 1866), Domenico Salvatori (1855-1909, admitted 1878) and Vincenzo Sebastianelli (1851-1919, admitted 1880). The original Papal Chapel Regulations of 1545 had established the duties of lead soprano, but none of these men were really capable of undertaking them. The most important stipulation was the singing of the soprano verses in the settings of the 'Miserere' sung during Holy Week. Cesari had succeeded Mustafà himself in this greatly-honoured role, but his voice had already shown signs of decline in the late 1870s.

Gustavo Pesci had the odd distinction of being the last of the Papal castrati not to have been born a Papal subject. He was a Florentine, and first saw service in the Chapel of the Grand Duke of Tuscany, Leopold II. He was appointed to the Sistine in 1855 as a *soprannumerario*. Citing 'family reasons', he returned to his native city after only eight months, but reapplied for admission on 22 December 1857, 'finding himself in an impoverished state'.

Pesci was already 50, and had only been admitted to the Sistine at the second attempt; Ritarossi was, on good authority, 'a choral soprano . . . of limited vocal gifts'.[64] Although he was Cesari's senior, Vissani had been passed over, while Salvatori, having started out as an alto, may never have acquired security in the required range. Sebastianelli, though the possessor of a high and powerful voice, seems to have been rather lacking in musical intelligence and to have had intonation problems. Moreschi's recent performance in *Cristo all' Uliveto* had demonstrated that he would have no trouble with any soprano solo, however stratospheric its tessitura, and so he was rapidly thrust into the limelight.

Except that his first solo appearance in the Sistine Chapel Choir was probably made in almost total darkness. The penitential psalm *Miserere mei, Deus* ('Have mercy upon me, O God'; number 51, or 50 in the Vulgate) has a considerable liturgical use, but to the lay person at least, the most memorable is that in the service known as *Tenebrae*

Moreschi at around the time of his entry into the Sistine Chapel Choir

('Darkness') just before the prayer at the end of the office of Lauds on Holy Wednesday, Maundy Thursday and Good Friday. At this point in the office all candles in the church, all six on the altar, and all but one of the fifteen on the Tenebrae hearse (a special type of triangular candelabrum) have been extinguished. The remaining one is hidden behind the altar, suitably providing the dimmest of illumination at a dark moment in the Christian calendar. Many composers have written settings of this psalm text, but the tradition of the Sistine Chapel was, typically, to use music by Sistine composers: on Wednesday by Giuseppe Baini, and on Thursday by Tommaso Bai (1650-1718), whose setting is similar to the most famous and oldest, that by Gregorio Allegri (1582-1652), a version of whose *Miserere* had been performed yearly since the late 1630s. It is Allegri's setting that has come to typify the secrecy surrounding the Sistine Chapel. Consisting as it does of repeated alternate verses of plainsong and relatively simple four-part harmony (a style called *falsobordone*),[65] the famous story of Mozart copying down the music at one hearing in 1770 is actually not at all hard to believe, and other musicians, notably Mendelssohn and the famous 18th-century historian Charles Burney, also made versions. However, few of the extant transcriptions from the 18th or 19th century include the lavish improvised ornamentation which was an intrinsic and very special part of the Sistine rendering, and it is probably a lack of knowledge outside the chapel of the Renaissance origins of these *abbellimenti* that gave rise to much of the piece's mystery.

By extraordinary coincidence, the date of the rescript admitting Moreschi to the Sistine in 1883 was also Maundy Thursday, just one day before Allegri's *Miserere* was to be performed there. Talented though he obviously was, Alessandro could not have simply jumped in to take the soloist's role. Though he might seem to have arrived in the nick of time, it is more likely that his appearance was the carefully-timed result of negotiation between Capocci, his *maestro* at the Lateran, and Mustafà, who probably gave him some prior coaching in his new role. Perhaps Alessandro, even when only a member of the Lateran choir, had been allowed to listen to previous performances, or sit in on rehearsals. Largely due to long-term problems of recruitment, by this date in the 19th century the once staunchly-defended lines of demarcation between the various Papal choirs had begun to break down.

As with many of the 'secrets' of the Sistine Chapel, there are conflicting reports of exactly which version of the *Miserere* was performed on which day. Sometimes at least, the versions performed were hybrids between all three composers' works. The version familiar to us nowadays[66] is a strange and musicologically dubious hybrid, little resembling anything ever performed in the Sistine in Moreschi's day or previously.

No doubt Mustafà impressed on the newcomer the importance of the tradition that was being entrusted to his voice. The two men seem to have been of very different character: Mustafà's brushes with authority and forceful reaction to the opposition of his colleagues would indicate a fiery and determined character, whereas Moreschi was referred to more than once as of a gentle, loving nature. Did Mustafà welcome him with open arms, or did he feel pangs of jealousy? There is certainly no surviving document, such as a letter from one to the other, containing any evidence of warmth between the two men. On the other hand, Mustafà was a strong upholder of the Sistine's special values, and would have understood that Alessandro was his only hope. The reaction of his new colleagues must also have been ambivalent: though they had called on him to audition to them in the first place, some feelings of envy at his rapid promotion would have been inevitable. He was the only one of the four last castrati to achieve full membership (*partecipante*) of the choir without the usual years of apprenticeship as a *soprannumerario*. The quality of his voice was clearly sufficient recommendation. The youngest of the castrati by some three years, his assumption of the role of first soprano soloist against all the hierarchical traditions of the Sistine Chapel would also have ruffled a few feathers of the other 'sacred capons' (as the Papal castrati had long been mockingly called). It was simply a matter of 'needs must …'

The quasi-gerontocratic nature of the body that Moreschi joined was just one of the various elements of the pre-1870 *ancien régime* that it retained. Though its increasingly large percentage of lay members may have seemed to make the status of the Cappella Musicale Pontificia as an 'ecclesiastical college' somewhat dubious, all of the singers were still eligible for minor orders (acolyte, lector, and the like): Alessandro was indeed still required, at least in form, to take the *prima tonsura* (the first stage in holy orders), and to undertake an obligation of celibacy. Castrati, incapable of procreation, had long been forbidden from marrying in any case, but some other Sistine singers had secretly married, even though discovery brought immediate expulsion. He was well within the choir's normal age-limit of 30 for admission, but he would have needed proof from his parish-priest in Montecompatri of his baptism and confirmation, as well as a certificate of good conduct from some suitably respectable person – perhaps from Maestro Capocci, who of course knew him well. Like all members of the Sistine Choir, he acquired the particular privilege of exemption from all fasts and abstinences ordained by the Church – perhaps it had originally been feared that any such penance would have threatened the singers' health, though by 1883 the workload was light enough to have been more likely to threaten laziness. In common with all Sistine singers admitted between 1870 and 1889 Moreschi had had no need to compete for his place, and in his case he had actually been invited to audition. Though he officially required the sanction of the choir-members to obtain admission, the request that he audition had probably come from Maestro Mustafà, and so their approval was almost certainly a foregone conclusion – one rather imagines that Mustafà liked to get his own way in such matters.

Having taken an oath of service on the Statutes of the Sistine Chapel, Alessandro was given what was termed 'life tenure' of his place, which in practical terms amounted to a fixed-term 30-year appointment, completion of which entitled him to a pension. At this ceremony he also received the 'cotta', an abbreviated surplice-like garment worn over the choir's regulation violet cassock (with crimson buttons) and sash:[67] except for the lack of a biretta, this was utterly priestly garb. The full uniform included a black silk cloak to be worn when not actually taking part in services; after 1871, this very clerical dress code had been relaxed for lay members of the choir, such as Moreschi, who were permitted to dress *in borghese* (in 'civvies') when not on duty. For his work in the Sistine

Chapel Alessandro was paid a monthly salary, which had been fixed in January 1871 at 118.25 *lire* for full members and 53.75 *lire* for supernumeraries; special services, such as funerals, paid extra. Official 'tips' were also doled out to each singer on the anniversary of the Pope's coronation (under Pius IX, 21 June, under Leo XIII, 3 March), on the feast of SS Peter and Paul (29 June), at Christmas, and at Easter.

The Sistine was not, of course, Moreschi's only source of income, and he would actually have had little opportunity to become lazy: he was already a regular 'guest' at the Cappella Giulia in St Peter's and had been granted official Papal leave to continue at the Cappella Pia (as the choir of St John Lateran was also known) 'until such time as the Palatine Chapels [which included the Sistine] shall be restored' (Papal rescript dated 31 March 1883[69]). There were

In 1900, a loaf of bread cost 38 *centesimi*, and a newspaper 5; a seat at La Scala 15 *lire*.[68] In 1913, the year of Moreschi's retirement, about 5 *lire* bought one US dollar, and 25 one pound sterling, the intervening period having been one of remarkable economic stability in developed countries.

large-scale architectural upheavals in the Vatican going on at this time, surrounding the reorganization of the Vatican Archives, and this served as the perfect pretext to assuage Maestro Capocci, who could hardly have been pleased to be losing his best soprano (probably, indeed, his only good one!) After all, it had been his idea to publicly show off Alessandro's voice in the first place.

Moreschi's youth and talent were certainly a vocal breath of fresh air at the Sistine Chapel, and a relief to those, like Mustafà, who were anxious about the continuity of its great traditions, but the young singer was becoming part of an establishment far bigger than any one singer. His role as saviour of the Allegri *Miserere*, though crucial, was only the most public part of his duties there.

Giovanni Pierluigi da Palestrina in an anonymous portrait of 1580

At the time of Moreschi's admission to the choir, the performing atmosphere within the Sistine was one of jealously guarded and unbroken tradition, dating back at least to the building of the chapel in the 15th century. In spite of changes in taste and musical style in the four intervening centuries, which had naturally affected actual performance practice, all members of the choir and of the Sistine establishment were immensely proud of what they regarded as the unchallengeable authenticity of their performances.

This was particularly true concerning the music of Palestrina, which dominated their polyphonic repertoire, as it had done for the three centuries since that composer's legendary saving of sacred music in face of the reforms demanded by the Council of Trent.

To modern ears, the name of Palestrina generally conjures up a sound-world of choirboy-led purity, devoted to loveliness of sound for its own sake, and largely without strong emotional involvement. Nothing could be further from the performance practice of the Sistine Choir during the latter half of the nineteenth century, not least because the sound of the castrato voice was a world away from that of the 'angelic' boy soprano (or of an adult woman, for that matter). The manner of their performance had been hedged about with secrecy and legend throughout the Sistine's existence, but a most useful guide to the choir's hidden practice is provided by a printed version of Palestrina's five-part motet *Peccavimus*, 'with the affects according to the tradition-

Giovanni Pierluigi da Palestrina (1525-1594) was perhaps the most famous Italian composer of the late Renaissance. A chorister at Santa Maria Maggiore, he was later *maestro di cappella* at St Peter's (from 1551 to 1555 and again from 1571). His 'Missa Papae Marcelli' acquired legendary status in supposedly saving church music from the reforms of the Council of Trent, but this story has now been discredited. His greatness as a composer cannot be doubted, however, though attempts at imitating his style, long regarded as the epitome of polyphonic purity, have been the bane of generations of music students.

al execution of the Sistine Chapel, notated accurately by Maestro Cavaliere Domenico Mustafà, Perpetual Director of the concerts of the said chapel, and President for Music in the Musical Society of Rome'. Published in 1878,[70] this edition is full of indications of dynamics (from *fortissimo* to *pianissimo*), crescendos and diminuendos, strong accents (called *il pichettare*) and *portamenti* (a superior form of glissando, 'carrying the voice' over an interval of several tones). The score is littered with romantic-sounding instructions like *sottovoce e legato* ('in an undertone and smoothly'), *con forza* ('with force') and *con slancio* ('dashingly' or 'with enthusiasm'). Strangest of all to the modern eye are the numerous additional anticipatory *acciaccature* (literally 'crushed notes') which are used to shift, and indeed distort, the work's written rhythmic notation. It should be borne in mind that part of the reason for such editorial additions would have been to make clear the various polyphonic lines in an echoing and obscuring acoustic. The effect produced would certainly have been oddly 'Romantic' to modern ears, some would say tasteless, but the validity of this centuries-old performance tradition cannot be dismissed out of hand. It was much closer to contemporary performances of opera than we might like to believe. Though Palestrina's original would have contained no such performance indicators, Moreschi and his colleagues would have regarded with incomprehension today's propensity for cleaning up so-called 'early music' in an effort to recreate its original sound world, and I feel sure would have found many modern renderings frigidly dull and inauthentic.

It is, however, also clear that this score does not tell the whole story (after all, no musical score ever can). The diaries and reports of earlier 19th-century visitors like the composers Otto Nicolai and Felix Mendelssohn refer to a practice of improvisatory embellishment of the written lines. This practice was current during Palestrina's own lifetime and was usually done *seriatim*, with no doubt the singers trying to outdo one another. Sometimes, however, several singers would improvise together, as Nicolai wrote: 'In the execution of the solos the Sistine singers take liberties so great that it is difficult to give an impression of them in relation to the score from which they are reading . . . moreover the singers, at their discretion, insert into the melody a multitude of embellishments, passing notes and slowings down . . . this addition of flourishes of every kind brings to the Sistine numerous distortions, and it must be admitted that nowadays many compositions become disfigured by unsuitable ornamentation . . . In any case, this practice of the Sistine, which is its most famous, is also its weakest . . . It is easy to understand that when diverse voices each adds passing notes in an arbitrary manner, the resultant harmony is unpleasant. I find particularly unbearable one figure, which is used to excess, and is moreover one of the principal ornaments of the newest Italian songs.'[71] However, the same writer also states: 'Most of the solos are executed in a manner so particular, so very beautiful, that it is truly indescribable!'[72]

To modern ears, the results of these long-standing conventions could seem extravagant, not to say chaotic. Unanimity in performance was not helped by all the singers reading, again as tradition dictated, from one very large score on a centrally-placed music-stand (from mid-century some pieces, especially newer entries to the repertoire, were written out on small sheets, perhaps in the hope that choir-members would take the trouble of learning something in their own time). Furthermore, the music itself was written in 'mensural' notation, full of open white notes of, to modern eyes, curious shape and grouping. This system had been current from the mid 13th-century until about 1600, but was uniquely old-fashioned by the 1880s. It was fortunate that many members of the choir had been singing the same repertoire for many years, since memory must have helped where visual contact was difficult or impossible. Mustafà's funerary monument in Montefalco, near Perugia, gives us a good impression of the choir grouped around their Director: he did not stand out front as is the modern way, with his back to the congregation, but rather, directed from a central position. It is indeed possible that he continued to sing while directing, not least because of the frequent lack of sopranos: the concept of the conductor as 'non-playing captain' is quite a recent one. (Not surprisingly, the monument, erected about 1912, displays artistic licence: none of the faces surrounding Mustafà resembles Moreschi in the least.)

The slack period of the 1870s had also seen many of the traditional performance practices described above fall into disuse, but Mustafà was determined to stage a revival. In 1884, he was able, with Moreschi as soloist, to rehearse a new score of the Bai-Allegri hybrid *Miserere,* his former rival Pasquali having been requested 'to write down [a version with] the ornaments, in order to assure and guarantee the real tradition . . . '[73]

As well as assimilating the Sistine choir's Palestrina style, Alessandro would have had to learn the remaining polyphonic repertoire. Some of this was by other well-known composers of the 16th to 18th centuries, such as Giovanni Anerio, Cristóbal Morales, Tomás Luis de Victoria, Benedetto Marcello and of course Allegri, whose *Miserere* was one of three of his works in the choir's repertoire at this period. However, there were as many scores by such obscure figures as Giovanni Fazzini, Filippo Ceciliani and Claudio Casciolini, who nowadays barely merit an entry in the largest of music dictionaries. Many of the works of baroque composers like Marcello and Casciolini were composed in a deliberately antique style known as the *prima prattica* (literally 'first practice') which imitated the manner of Palestrina, though not always completely avoiding more contemporary stylistic traits.

Without any desire or perceived need for an historicist approach to performance, this whole repertoire would have been sung in the full-blown Romantic manner of the late 19th century. Moreschi's voice was part of a tradition stretching back to the time of Palestrina, and so he would have seen nothing wrong in performing that composer's music in a manner similar to that used when singing the works of living or recently deceased composers like Verdi or Rossini. He would also have sung a considerable amount of modern repertoire: at the Sistine this was dominated by the music of those present and past Directors of the choir Giuseppe Baini (36 entries in the catalogue) and Mustafà (18), with several contributions also from others associated with the chapel, such as Pasquali (nine entries), Mariano Astolfi (six), Emilio Calzanera, and Domenico Costantini. Here there was also a definite mix between music carrying on the *prima prattica* tradition more or less strictly (like that of Pasquali) and that including elements of a more contemporary pseudo-operatic style, as did many of Baini's and Mustafà's works. In 1886, when the senior castrato Cesari retired, Moreschi probably took over as Director of Soloists (*Direttore dei concertisti*), an important role, since there were frequent solo passages for one or more voices in all of this repertoire, as well as a tradition of contrasting solo and full forces in the earlier music.

As lead soprano, Moreschi also had a vital part to play in the choir's most ancient repertoire: Gregorian chant, an enormous corpus of largely early melodies used to sing the various parts of the Church's liturgy. Tradition was that it had originated with Pope Gregory I ('the Great', reigned 590-604). The long-standing peculiarities of the Sistine Chapel's performance of chant were well attested, and not always in complimentary terms - in a letter to his family dated 4 April 1831, Mendelssohn had written: 'they must scream the Psalms as loudly as possible, and moreover always on one note, on which the words are spoken at great speed.'[74] Under the rules of the *Constitutiones Cappellae Pontificiae* the senior soprano was responsible for leading all the versicles and responses of the office, but in the Sistine Chapel at this time these had little similarity to what may be familiar to us today from, say, an Anglican cathedral evensong. Moreschi would have had to learn, for example, the Sistine manner of ornamenting all the cadence-points of these (and all other) chant melodies, and also the chapel practice of *contrappunto alla mente*, a semi-improvised technique of performing chant in a harmonised form. This involved cloaking the chant melody in others extemporised at certain fixed harmonic intervals, rather in the manner of what is known as *fauxbourdon*. Again it should be remembered that the sound of this during Moreschi's time in the choir would have borne little relation to the clean-cut performances of medieval repertoire that became customary in the historically-informed performances of the last quarter of the 20th century, or to the otherworldly solemnity of much recent singing of liturgical chant - standard modern conceptions of performing this repertoire really date from the reforms of the Benedictine monks of Solesmes, whose theory and practice of singing Gregorian chant did not become dominant in Rome until the turn of the century.

In spite of Mustafà's avowed desire to reinvigorate the choir's activities, during Moreschi's early years at the Sistine Chapel any efforts in this regard seem to have proceeded by fits and starts. The chronic problem of recruitment remained: had the Sistine Choir ever been at its official full strength of 32, Mustafà might have felt himself rather crowded in the chapel's relatively small

Pope Leo XIII was an aristocrat who for 25 years never spoke to his coachman, and was widely known as *Il Papa-Re* (The Pope King). He sure-footedly walked a political tightrope throughout his pontificate and thus restored the papacy's prestige in the world, though his dreams of being a key mediator in world affairs were never realised. He reaffirmed the Scholastic doctrine that Science and Religion could co-exist, opened up the Vatican archives to researchers, including Protestants, and recognised the French Republic. On the other hand he condemned freemasonry, capitalism and communism, and declared Anglican holy orders null and void. He famously also publicly endorsed a popular commercial concoction of the day known as 'Vin Mariani', a hugely successful mixture of wine and cocaine, whose devotees included Queen Victoria.

An advertisement for Vin Mariani
as endorsed by Pope Leo XIII

choir-loft, but in actual fact this was rarely the case during his whole tenure of office. In 1883, when Moreschi was one of five new members admitted by papal rescript, the Sistine Diaries record that there were altogether only 19 active members of the choir. Except for Moreschi, these five all had to submit to a period of probation, which shows how determined Mustafà was to raise standards. By 1889 indeed, he was confident enough to return to the system of admission by public competition, thus at least giving the impression that a place in the Sistine Choir was once more something to be vied for. This may have been bravura on his part, since throughout the 1880s there is increasing evidence of singers from each of the papal basilicas performing at any and all of the others, in a spirit both of informal cooperation and probably to keep up numbers in each place. Because of this, there was much concern that the homogeneity and special characteristics of the Sistine Choir's mode of performance would be lost, and frequent appeals were made to the Holy Father for new appointments. The reply to this came in 1887, and not as was hoped: instead, the prefects of the three basilicas were ordered to contact one another to organise a regular system of singing deputies. Rivalry between the basilicas had always existed, and this new set-up could only have increased tensions, with the poor singers feeling perhaps rather like many a present-day Anglican Vicar in a rural area rushing between the widely spread-out services of a doctrinally varied multiple benefice.

Such uncertainties clearly took their toll: between 1883 and 1887, according to the Sistine Diaries, the *Direttore generale in perpetuo* was frequently absent, retreating in times of adversity to his home town of Montefalco and leaving the direction of the choir in the hands of his old adversary Pasquali. He even attempted to resign on two occasions. Clearly, like the Pope himself, who famously brooked no contradiction, Mustafà hated to be crossed, but he did have the political sense to make timely reappearances. A notable example of this came at Leo's *Messa d'oro* ('Golden Mass'), marking the *Giubileo* (50th anniversary) of his ordination. At this Mass, on 1 January 1888, Mustafà conducted the first performance of his motet *Dominum salvum me fac*. I should imagine Pasquali was livid, since this was Mustafà's first appearance in the chapel for months.

The indefatigable Mrs de Hegemann-Lindencrone was again present: 'MY DEAR AUNT, - Leo XIII's jubilee has been the means of bringing the world to Rome . . . On last Thursday the Pope said Mass in St Peter's. It was the great event of the year . . . I cannot honestly say the music was beautiful. With the exception of the days when the best singers of the Pope's choir perform, the music in St Peter's is not good.'[75] How that would have annoyed Maestro Meluzzi, Moreschi's old adversary, and conductor of the main choir at St Peter's. The fact is that by this date all the Masters of Music of the three papal basilicas were men in their

Moreschi in a group photograph of the Sistine
choir dating from the late 1880s

seventies, probably rather stuck in their ways, and certainly tired.
Mustafà, by contrast, was a sprightly 60-year old

These celebrations formed something of a climax to the Sistine
Choir's increased activities during the 1880s, which had continued
to be plagued by money problems stemming from the papacy's
uncertain financial state. (Pius IX and Leo had both refused the
annual income of 3.5 million Lire offered by the new Italian government as compensation for the loss of the Papal States, preferring

The medal Pro Ecclesia et Pontefice

to rely on donations from the church itself.) At least all the members of the choir received the silver version of the papal medal *Pro Ecclesia et Pontefice* ('For Church and Pontiff') struck to commemorate the occasion.

They would probably have preferred a rise, since even those with a high public profile like Moreschi were still not permitted to take part in paid concerts. Nonetheless, having now established himself at the pinnacle of Rome's ecclesiastical music hierarchy, Alessandro also found time to appear in the best singing company and the most elevated secular society: 'At the Hotel Russia[76] he sang alongside the tenor Francesco Marconi (a favourite of Mascagni, composer of *Cavalleria Rusticana*) and the baritone Antonio Cotogni, an artist much admired by Giuseppe Verdi. The famous soprano [Marie] Durand, who should have taken part in the concert, did not wish to participate, fearing the comparison …'[77] (a report of a private concert perhaps held in 1889, when Cotogni, at the height of his international career, was appearing at the Rome Opera House). What dramatic Verdian trios or blood-curdling *verismo* scenes these singers may have performed together is not known, and the effect can only be imagined – Madame Durand may have been frightened of being measured against Moreschi, but Marconi had probably never even heard a castrato. Cotogni, at least, would not have found the experience totally strange: he had performed with Moreschi before, and in his 1851 debut, at the church of Santa Maria in Valicella, he had sung with Mustafà himself. This was just the sort of occasion on which

Moreschi might have let himself go, and performed items known to have been favourites of his: 'O mio Fernando', a dramatic mezzo-soprano aria from Donizetti's *La Favorita,* or numbers from the hugely demanding coloratura role of Abigaille in Verdi's *Nabucco.*[78] If he could bring these off, and his reputation as 'The Angel of Rome' would suggest that he could, no wonder Madame Durand preferred to stay in her dressing-room!

Although the style is of course completely different, Moreschi's venturing into mezzo repertoire is reminiscent of earlier castrati's abilities to sing an enormous gamut of pitches – the great Farinelli, for example, had a range of over three octaves, and his arias are full of passages that plunge vertiginously from high soprano to tenor, and back. The drama of Abigaille's outbursts are also a far cry from the graceful glitter of Marguerite's *Jewel Song,* so Moreschi, still only about 30, was clearly maturing into an artist capable of a wide emotional range.

All the opera repertoire Moreschi is known to have sung was written originally for women to perform, which perhaps seems odd to us. Indeed we could justifiably wonder at his ability to truly convey any intrinsic femininity in the music, and be tempted to draw psycho-sexual inferences about the singer from his choice of it. I believe this is a false trail: it needs to be remembered that he really had no option, since the castrato repertoire of the eighteenth century was completely forgotten by the 1880s. The serious operas of Rossini, like *Tancredi* or *La Donna del Lago,* with 'pseudo-castrato' male roles originally sung by women *en travesti,* were also totally out of fashion. By the late 19th century the denizens of Rome's fashionable and aristocratic salons would have found the florid baroque style of the earlier century antiquated and dull, and really only knew Rossini as a composer of comedy – the last thing Moreschi dared do was bore his wealthy patrons with the unfashionable or the antique.

The Years of
the new Constitution 1891-1898

As well as his increased responsibilities and high public profile
as a singer, Moreschi was also about to assume two important
administrative posts at the Sistine Chapel, at a time of great
importance and of great crisis in that institution's long history.
In 1891, at the age of 32, he was elected *segretario-puntatore*. As
holder of this post, he was responsible for keeping records of all
the choir's activities, both in the Sistine and elsewhere. He also
had to record the 'black marks', known as *punti,* noted against an
individual singer's name for infringements of the choir rules,
which covered matters as various as unexplained absence and the
singing of wrong notes. These he kept in *quinternetti*, small note-
books, traditionally of five sheets, which were handed on for official transcription by the next *segretario*: a potentially rich source
of bribery and corruption, since there were often fines to pay for
rule-breaking, and perhaps next year's secretary might be persuaded to forget one or two.

The 'crisis' was, not surprisingly, centred around Mustafà,
who, having turned up in order to upstage Pasquali in January
1888, promptly disappeared again for a seemingly indefinite period. He seems not to have been convinced that he was getting sufficient support for the reforms of the choir's practice and organisation that he wished to see. On 21 January 1891, the Sistine
Diaries, Moreschi's responsibility during this year, recorded that
*it has been decided unanimously to write to maestro Mustafà, begging him
to take up his duties again.*[79] Moreover, the situation had 'put the

Chapel into a serious state of embarrassment, threatening its final demise'. Members of the College were apparently considering 'turning to foreign directors to succeed Mustafà, and that, in order not to besmirch the good name of Italy.'[80] This rather curious phraseology, from a journalist and scholar who knew the workings of the Sistine chapel as well as any outsider could, implies that the members of the choir knew of no other Roman or Italian, Pasquali included, whom they wished to entrust with the post of Director. Such incipient fears for the future were well grounded.

On 23 January the necessary letter was sent to the absent Director by Monsignor Ruffo Scilla, Prefect of the Papal Palaces who, as major-domo to the Pope, was in overall charge of the Sistine Chapel. He strongly supported Mustafà's reform plans ('it was he who by his tenacity achieved the implementation of the project of the Signor Director'[81]) and acted as intermediary between the choir, the Pope, and the Vatican authorities. Considering how traditional Mustafà had always been, some of the eventual reforms are perhaps surprising, since they certainly contain an element of moving with the times. Obviously the new regulations did not flow from his pen alone. Another letter from Scilla to the *maestro pro tempore* Vincenzo Sebastianelli[82] shows that the Vatican was adopting something of a carrot-and-stick approach to the whole matter since, as well as outlining various modernising moves and easings of restrictions, it also admonished the papal singers to keep closely to the Sistine's great traditions, implying in addition that the diligence of some choir members in carrying out their duties was not all that it might have been: 'sanctions will be established against those singers who show that they have forgotten what may be demanded of them in return for the salaries which they receive.' Scilla also informs the choir that twice monthly public performances by the choir are to be reinstated (he uses the word *accademia* here, which should be taken in its broadest sense of 'meeting of a learned society'). These were to take place in the vicinity of the Vatican, so that resident priests could form the audience and give encouragement. The season for the *accademie* would run from the beginning of November until the end of June, which would at least permit prelates and singers alike to escape from Rome for the traditionally long Italian summer holiday. (The city had long been regarded as uninhabitable during the hot months of the year, not least because of the threat of malaria.)

Clearly, Moreschi's little book of black marks had been filling up all too quickly, but the letter also contains an element of 'letting the singers know what they were in for' - not strictly necessary, but politically astute. Mustafà's return had also been successfully smoothed. The Sistine Diary for 2 March recorded that on his reappearance in front of his colleagues *much moved, he saluted and thanked the entire College for the letter sent to him, but said that he could not promise to remain at the head of the said College because of his uncertain state of health, and were he in addition not to receive the support of his superiors for the reordering and returning of the Chapel to the glory which for many years it had deservedly possessed.*[83]

Perhaps Mustafà was still not sure that he would get the said support from above, but on March 7 Pope Leo signed a decretal (papal letter carrying legal force) ushering in a new Constitution (here termed a *Regolamento)* for the Sistine choir.[84] One important effect of the new rules was to reduce significantly the clerical nature of the whole establishment. It would no longer be necessary to take the *prima tonsura* nor generally to wear any clerical dress, except when on duty, and the old obligation to celibacy was also removed. This latter was referred to in a most curious way: 'chapter 1 [section] d: For those singers, *who are not otherwise constrained* [my italics], the obligation to celibacy, common to all salaried members, is revoked'. Some members of the choir were still priests, whose celibate status could not, of course, be overturned, but the originally italicised phrase about constraint can also be seen as a reference to the castrati - in the eyes of the Catholic church non-procreative sex was (and still is) taboo. Along with the possibility that lay members of the choir could marry, they were also to be permitted to carry on another profession, while each singer's monthly salary was to be raised to 140 *lire*. Furthermore, the choir was to return to its original full strength of 32, no longer including the retired members. Earlier in the century, when problems of recruitment had been particularly acute, the retired had had to be included to make up a semblance of sufficient numbers. The new stipulation implied a need and a desire for further recruitment, and was also directly linked to the most radical of the new constitution's provisions: the additional admission, at last, of boys

A photograph of Mustafà in 1898, the 50th year of his association with the Sistine choir

from the Pontifical School of San Salvatore in Lauro as full members of the choir. Four of the most experienced boys would be taken on and trained by the *maestro pro tempore* (in this year, that post was held by the castrato Sebastianelli – one wonders what the boys' reaction to him was). Pupils from the Gregorian School of Santa Maria dell'Anima were also to be brought in as reinforcements (This first happened, appropriately enough, at the festivities marking the 13th centenary of Pope Gregory the Great's consecration on 10 April 1891.) Another new regulation was that absentees would have to be replaced by others of the same voice from another of the papal basilicas – in the castrati's case this was no longer possible, so one must infer that boys would have taken over. The resultant psychological difference to the choir's sound would have been even greater than the merely aural. The new rules also imply that the authorities recognised that even the new monthly salary might not be sufficient, since secular members of the choir were permitted to enter a profession of their choice, as long as this received official approval.[85]

There was one big problem with these reforms: they did not take immediate effect, perhaps because of the intractability of Vatican bureaucracy. The non-appearance of new recruits was particularly disappointing: Moreschi notes in the Diary that when the choir travelled to Orvieto on 15 August to celebrate the feast of the Assumption, its numbers were perforce supplemented by singers from the Cappella Giulia and by other 'additional invitees'. Mustafà was worried that this was compromising the standard of performance he wished to attain, and in November he retreated again to Montefalco. Once more his return was only secured by the intervention of the Pope's long-suffering major-domo Ruffo Scilla.

In 1892, as was customary after serving as *segretario-puntatore*, Moreschi was elected to another important choir office, that of *maestro pro tempore*. It is a curiosity of Sistine history that though strictly organised on a 'top down' basis, the choir should hold secret ballots for these two posts, but such was the case, and always had been - democracy by tradition! Although the title of Moreschi's new position literally translates as 'master as the occasion requires', it did not involve any conducting, but was chiefly administrative, being concerned with calling choir meetings, fixing rehearsals, granting leave of absence and the like. During this year, Alessandro was also responsible for overseeing the choir's correct carrying-out of its duties in the Sistine Chapel. Artistically speaking, the job involved him in choosing soloists (himself included, one supposes) and in developing repertoire: he was entitled to suggest new pieces and have copies made for the archives. In this regard, there is clear evidence of a collaboration between Moreschi and Mustafà, and of a happy coincidence between their respective abilities as performer and composer: 'The Maestro Director presents his afore-mentioned Miserere, a work which has cost him many years of patient toil in order to transmit to posterity the manner in which it came to be executed; and modestly demands of his colleagues, turning particularly to those of some seniority who remember former performances, freely to disclose their opinion of the said work, saying that he was ready to remove those flaws and to make redress for those omissions into which he may have fallen. The senior members, and with them the whole College, approve of this valuable work by its illustrious Director; and the maestro pro-tempore [Moreschi] speaks on behalf of the most reverend College as a whole in thanking him for this work of his given to the Chapel.'

This entry in the Sistine Diaries for 8 March 1892[86] recorded an occasion when, at a rehearsal of the Bai-Allegri *Miserere*, Mustafà presented the choir with his own version of this work, incorporating all the ornamentation that he knew and had sung himself in his younger days, and which he had passed on to Moreschi almost a decade previously. Perhaps Alessandro persuaded his illustrious predecessor to bring this work to fruition, and thus perpetuate in written form a memory of their joint performances. Mustafà's score is full of performance directions, some of which directly relate to Moreschi's singing: 'as the 1st soprano wishes', 'hold until the 1st soprano resolves [the harmony]', 'if it suits the 1st soprano better to support the high G he may first take the middle G'[87]. About one aspect of his new version Mustafà was distinctly nervous - at the head of his manuscript score, dedicated to Pope Leo XIII and dated 23 January 1892, he wrote: . . . Miserere by Bai and Allegri. In which are noted the work's traditional mode of performance in the Sistine by the Singers of the Papal

Chapel. Owing to unfortunate interruptions to the continuity of papal ceremonial in consequence of which much may be forgotten, I, the writer, after forty-five years passed amongst my dear colleagues in the service of God, the Supreme Pontiff and the Chapel, have thought to transcribe the above-mentioned traditions (in so far as I could), as much for those who must conduct as for the solo singers, so that after many years the effects which made the Sistine performance so renowned should not be lost.' It is his postscript which is most revealing: 'On behalf of the College of the Papal Singers I beg the Supreme Pontiff that he should not permit the making of copies. . . .'[88] The Sistine tradition of secrecy was clearly still very much alive.

Mustafà also remained prickly on the subject of the number of singers at his disposal. In June 1892 he is recorded in the Sistine Diary as having communicated to the choir: 'that it is very likely that they will in all probability not perform at services in the venerable basilica of St Peter's, he having remarked to his superiors that the Pontifical Chapel, having itself so small a number of members, could not show itself as decorum demands . . . '. Stating that he was in poor health, he also repeated that he felt forced to withdraw from his *terzo servizio* contract (due to end the next year), and remarked that he did not wish 'to draw the salary without the respect that went with it'. The singers seem to have become rather tired of his capriciousness, since the Diary states at this point that they decided not to argue with him any longer.[89]

Though unsurprisingly no records remain, one can well imagine Moreschi, as a senior choir official, having long and probably difficult talks with his crotchety Director during these months. In this fraught atmosphere, he was no doubt glad of an opportunity to escape from his duties for once: in August 1892 the citizens of his home town of Montecompatri celebrated the 25th anniversary of their deliverance from the 1867 cholera epidemic, which, as has I have already suggested, may, in one way or another, have started the singer's career. A papal decree of 21 June granted indulgences to all who went to venerate the image of the Madonna del Castagno between August 14 and 30 September. The town authorities were keen to see their famous son return, if briefly: on 21 August 'under the direction of Professor Alessandro Moreschi, native of this town, there took place a most solemn mass, the music directed by him, and performed by twelve distinguished professors from the capital, and moreover by pupils from the school of San Salvatore in Lauro; and, in the evening there was Vespers, during which was sung the famous Laudate Pueri by Maestro Capocci with the choir of boys.'[90] This last-named work was written by Moreschi's former teacher and choir-master in 1856, and set for tenor, boys' choir, and orchestra – perhaps Moreschi had some fun and took over the tenor soloist's role, singing it up the octave.

Domenico Mustafà

During the celebrations there was a furious squabble between the townsfolk and the Carmelite Friars of San Salvatore – the two services had taken place in the parish church of the Annunciation in the centre of the town, whereas the monastics had wanted them celebrated in the monastery. This wasn't just a matter of who would have to walk further, but was, rather, part of a long-running controversy over the jurisdiction over the chapel of the Madonna del Castagno and its holy image.

A depiction of the 23rd meeting of the Council of Trent
(once attributed to Titian)

From what may well have been Alessandro's first return home
for over twenty years we have no record of the responses of his
family, friends and neighbours to their distinguished, if strange-
sounding fellow townsman. No more are Moreschi's own feelings
recorded, so whether his home town now seemed a tranquil retreat
or merely a narrow provincial backwater full of bickering locals can
only be surmise. He was at least accustomed to ecclesiastical backbiting. He had also somehow managed to get leave from the Sistine
chapel on a Sunday, not just for himself but for another 'twelve
distinguished professors', some of whom were sure to have been
singers there, or at one of the Papal basilicas - perhaps he used his
status as *maestro pro tempore* to pull rank, or more likely the authorities in Rome, who would have known all about the Madonna del
Castagno because of the long-standing links between her cult and
the Papacy, realised just how important the celebrations were.

Back in Rome there was more than backbiting to contend

with. Musicological storm-clouds of an increasingly lowering hue were brewing which would have a profound effect on the last thirty years of Moreschi's life, and bring Mustafà's long career to a troubled end. As is customary, this slow-brewing hurricane had a name: *Cäcilianismus*. This 'Cecilian movement' took its name from the patron-saint of music, St Cecilia, and from the 15th-century Italian *Congregazioni Ceciliani* (religious communities devoted to the cult of the saint). These latter had in turn in-spired the 18th-century Cecilian

The Council of Trent was the 19th ecumenical council of the Roman Catholic Church. Its deliberations lasted from 13 December, 1545 until 4 December, 1563, and their main object was to determine definitively Catholic doctrine in answer to the Protestant Reformation which had been sweeping northern Europe, especially during the previous two decades. The Council also proposed a thorough reform of the inner life of the Catholic Church by removing the numerous abuses that had developed in it, which had been greatly derided by Martin Luther and his fellow reformers.

Leagues in such cities as Munich, Passau and Vienna, which were organisations of church musicians dedicated to the upholding of an ideal of sacred music, epitomised by monophonic plainchant and the polyphony of Palestrina. These regarded few accompanying instruments other than the organ as liturgically acceptable, and held that church music was to be at the service of the liturgy, rather than important in an artistically independent sense.

There is virtually nothing here that should have caused controversy in the Catholic Church of Moreschi's day, since such a line of thought was directly derived from the provisions of the Council of Trent in the 16th century.

Theoretically the Church's music was still bound by these 'Tridentine' rules, but there was a wide divergence between what had been laid down on paper (or parchment) and what had actually occurred in the succeeding three centuries. The very presence

Lithurgical neglect was widespread in 16th-century Catholicism: 'Finding myself once on a journey, I was given hospitality by a noble and very rich bishop; I saw his palace resplendent with vases of silver and his table smothered in the most exquisite viands. Also all the rest was spick and span and the napkins richly perfumed. But the day after, going down early in the morning into the church attached to his palace to celebrate the sacred rites, I encountered a total contrast: all was mean and disgusting, so much so that I had to do myself violence in order to dare to celebrate the Divine Mysteries in such a place and with such apparatus'.[92]

ROBERT CARDINAL BELLARMINE
(1542-1621)

of the castrati was symptomatic of the fact that the basic human desire for sensual gratification (whether achieved aurally or otherwise) could, and often did, override moral distaste or the dictates of Canon Law. Secular musical styles of the intervening centuries had also invaded church composition, and there was little that even Papal pronouncements could do about it. During the 17th century, Alexander VII and Innocent XI tried to rein things in, but it was Benedict XIV's encyclical *Annus qui hunc* of 1749, which, in attempting to clean up more or less everything concerning the rites of the church, made the most determined efforts at control.[91] Though admitting to having had no musical training himself, the Pope there naturally quoted at great length from earlier theological authorities in an effort to prescribe what is and is not acceptable as music in the context of Christian ritual. He speaks highly of Gregorian plainchant, particularly recommending its monastic practitioners, but then seems to get in rather a tangle as he tries to formulate his position, falling back frequently on remarks about 'songs which are completely unsuitable to the sacred mysteries of the church'. He is particularly exercised by singers trilling to excess and extended musical settings that hold up the course of the mass; he decides that bassoons and violins might just be permitted to play in church, but that drums, trumpets, mandolins and harps are too 'theatrical'. I wonder what King David would have made about this last exclusion, particularly since the Pope permitted *la cetra* – either a zither or Apollo's lyre! One problem here is that, had Pope Benedict's strictures been successfully applied, the masses of Haydn and Mozart, amongst many others, would never have been written.

A revived Cecilian movement in the early 19th century centring on the Catholic areas of Southern Germany cited Benedict's encyclical as an authority for the removal of virtually all instruments from church music, and, in a spirit of nostalgia typical of a society in the early stages of industrialization, looked back on composers of the late Renaissance, and especially Palestrina, as models of purity and simplicity. Any elements perceived as 'theatrical', such as overly graphic word-painting or 'emotional' chromaticism were eschewed as anathema. Thus, as well as the sacred music of these Viennese masters, the Cecilianists sought to write off such masterpieces as Beethoven's *Missa Solemnis,* Handel's *Dixit Dominus* and Vivaldi's *Gloria.*

To further Cecilian ideals, church choirs modelled on the Sistine Chapel choir were set up in Munich, Cologne and Regensburg (though hardly exact models – there had been no castrati performing in Germany since about 1800). An important Cecilianist figure at this time was the Silesian Karl Proske (1794-1861) who, having been trained as a doctor, was ordained priest in 1826, and soon after became a vicar choral (member of the choir) of the cathedral in Regensburg, becoming a canon and Master of the Music there in 1830. He was fortunate to possess a private income, and for the rest of his life devoted himself to the compilation of two huge collections of what he termed *polyphoniam vere ecclesiasticam* ('true ecclesiastical polyphony'): *Musica Divina* (four volumes, published 1853-63) and *Selectus Novus Missarum* (two volumes, 1856-61), both of which included only included 'suitable' music in the Palestrina style. His introduction to the former work includes an excellent, if rather sententious, distillation of the entire ethos of *Cäcilianismus*, revealing its highly conservative Catholic basis: 'Art, torn asunder from the depths of belief, from the severity of truth and of life, and from faithfulness to the Church – what exaltation can it perform, what reward can it offer, what consolation can it afford?'[93] To collect Renaissance repertoire and hear the works of composers such as Palestrina and Victoria in 'authentic' performance he travelled to Italy between 1834 and 1838, and especially to Rome.

Proske's reports of what he heard in the Sistine chapel were later used as ammunition in a increasing attack on the performance traditions of that august institution, which had hitherto been greatly honoured by musicians, not least because of their unbroken nature. A follower of Proske, Father Franz Xaver Witt (1834-88), who had founded the *Allgemeiner Deutscher Cäcilienverein* ('General German Cecilian Union') in 1868, wrote: 'It is not true that the Sistine or rather Mustafà held to the tradition 'truly from the baton of Palestrina' to the present. The descriptions relayed to me by Proske of the Sistine under Baini, are as far from the direction of Mustafà as genius is from artisanship'.[94] As well as being the first Perpetual Director of the Sistine choir, Baini was well-known for his monumental biography of Palestrina, which of course helped to give him impeccable Cecilianist credentials. However, Witt is being very naïve here, only believing what he wants to believe: the reports of Sistine performances of Palestrina and his contemporaries during the 1830s by eminent musicians like Nicolai and Mendelssohn show that the traditions of ornamentation and suchlike were if anything more prevalent under Baini than under Mustafà. In spite of Baini's own devotion to Palestrina, his own compositions were by no means strictly imitative of him; some were in the *stile antico*, as it was known, but many others have a distinct flavour of Rossini or Donizetti, which, considering when he was writing is hardly surprising. Clearly Witt's attack on Sistine traditions was being made under false pretences, employing a common historicist premise of preferring 'how things were done then', even though he was in this case mistaken about that as well.

The problem from Mustafà's point-of-view was that Cecilianism had also, by the 1880s, got up a considerable head of steam in Italy. This had come about within a general political climate in which a newly-active lay Catholicism, setting itself against what it saw as the anti-church policies of the secular government, had founded such organisations as the *Opera dei Congressi e de Comitati Cattolici*, the first congress of which took place in Venice in 1874. Similarly, in Milan, on 4 September 1880 the first *Congresso Nazionale Ceciliano* was held, founding the *Associazione Italiana di Santa Cecilia.* It is interesting to note that both of these organisations originated in northern Italy; the desire of the 'progressive' North of the country to show the 'supposedly backward' South, Rome included, 'how things should be done' is very much alive to this day.

But Cecilianism had also reached the heart of Western Christianity, where, though it encountered the ultra-conservative Pope Pius IX, it could base its validity on the inviolable pre-scriptions of the Council of Trent, not to mention even earlier religious authority. In 1868, Rome sanctioned a new edition of Gregorian chant produced in Regensburg, while in 1870 the Pope had given Witt's Union his blessing. In 1884, Cecilianism was officially legalised within the church by the Congregation of Sacred Rites (the body controlling liturgy in the Catholic Church) in its 'Regulations Concerning Sacred Music.[95] That year had also seen the founding of the *Union de Fribourg*, a forum for Catholic social thinkers from France, Belgium, Germany, Switzerland and Austria as well as Italy. This body was very influential on Pope Leo's thinking on social questions, which were exemplified in his most famous encyclical *Rerum Novarum,* a seminal document for the Church's attitude to problems of modern industrial society. This *rapprochement* with the contemporary world was to have serious concomitant effects on the Church's music, for all that Cecilianism itself was essentially a backward-looking movement. As to Gregorian chant, there was also a long-standing conflict between traditional performance exemplified by the Sistine Chapel and two differing conceptions of using early manuscript sources. Haberl's 1868 revision of the Medicean edition of Gregorian chant was still officially recognised, but by the 1890s was under considerable criticism from scholarly and ecclesiastical figures supporting the work of the monks of Solesmes under Dom Pothier and Dom Mocquereau, whose more radical attitude eventually triumphed. It is interesting to note the French Benedictines' positive response to the Sistine Choir's performance of polyphony, while they decry its singing of chant. In February 1890[96], Dom Mocquereau attended the funeral of Cardinal Giuseppe Pecci, the Pope's brother, at the basilica of the Santissimi Apostoli: 'We heard the Sixtine Chapel . . . by my side Father de Santi and the son of General Kanzler, a plainchant scholar . . . The voices were magnificent and the music was executed with absolute perfection, but the plainsong was hammered, thumped out in an ugly manner, and shouted; one could not believe that these were the same artists . . . '[97] there would seem to be a certain amount of scholarly tunnel vision here (or 'tunnel hearing', if such a mixed metaphor be permitted – Mocquereau praises just what the Cecilianists were execrating). Baron Rodolfo Kanzler (1864-1924), was an adviser to the Pontifical School of Sacred Music and Professor of Gregorian Chant at the Accademia di Santa Cecilia, who also attacked the Sistine's 'abuse of embellishment'[98] in performing polyphony. Father Angelo de Santi was the editor of the influential Jesuit journal *Civiltà Cattolica*, and became an influential supporter of the Solesmes position, while giving frequent voice to reformers' concerns about the Sistine choir as a whole.[99]

By 1892 the Cecilianist approach to church music and the continuous tradition exemplified by the Sistine Chapel were heading for direct conflict. Mustafà himself was certain of the rightness of his approach. Rehearsing Palestrina's 'Lamentations' ' . . . he went back to the traditional manner, the performance of which was applauded by all, especially the senior members, who remembered the old way . . .'[100] The rehearsal referred to here took place during Advent 1892, not the liturgical season for lamentation, so Mustafà clearly took seriously the need for rehearsal and generally keeping everyone up to the mark. He and the Sistine Choir clearly also enjoyed strong personal support from the Pope: 'At the Sistine, a rehearsal of the motets 'Sancte Michael' and 'Oremus pro Pontefice' by Mustafà. Some additional *professori* and the boys from San Salvatore in Lauro took part . . . the singers went to wait upon the Holy Father in the Sala Clementina and took up a position to the right by the great door leading to the Scala Regia. At 12.40 the Holy Father, on his portable throne and accompanied by members of his Noble Guard, entered the room and sat upon another throne especially erected at the far end opposite the principal entrance. On an order from His Holiness, the Oremus and Sancte Michael were performed, at the end of which a gentleman-in-waiting to His Holiness presented himself to the Director in order to invite him to approach the foot of the throne. At the same moment the Holy Father arose and came to meet the Director near the singers. Clasping him repeatedly by the hand, while [the Director] bowed to kiss the [Fisherman's] ring, he congratulated him warmly for the fine performance, and more especially for his new composition: "I am happy to express to maestro Mustafà the pleasure I take in his most beautiful music". His Holiness was gracious enough to address other words of good will and encouragement to the performers while they knelt to kiss the sacred ring. "I impart", said the Holy Father, "my apostolic blessing to you all, and especially to maestro Mustafà". The Director, profoundly moved, replied, "Holiness, I am old!" Emotion was on the faces of all present. . . .'[101]

Though the scene described here is one stiff with a sense of hierarchy and tradition, it is perhaps all the more notable that the Pope breaks with his own protocols to show personal human warmth to a valued servant, the quality and manner of whose work he obviously appreciates. His Holiness was also pleased with his own handiwork, having written the words to 'Sancte Michael' himself. The work's first public performance was on 3 March 1892, the 24th anniversary of his coronation. In the following years it was one of the most frequently performed pieces in the whole Sistine Chapel repertoire – Mustafà clearly realised the value of appealing to Papal vanity.

In the north of Italy, meanwhile, rigidities of another kind were being formulated: [letter dated]12 October 'I have presented to each of the right reverend bishops here assembled a copy of the statutes of the Lombardy Regional Society of Saint Gregory, and all have applauded the zeal which animates it, in conformity with the spirit of the Church and with the recent prescriptions of the Holy See, to promote the study and performance of sacred music, one of the main parts of the liturgy, which so much encourages and maintains true devotion among the faithful. [The Society] may be quite certain, that in the sacrifices it makes, including that of printing the periodical 'The Venetian School of Sacred Music', it will enjoy the undiminished support and protection of us all: support and protection which are elsewhere confirmed by those invited [here], whose duty it is to give special direction to those clerics in our seminaries, where in accordance with pontifical prescriptions the teaching of sacred music is encouraged. And with such a declaration, which will be to you I hope no small encouragement, I am pleased to subscribe myself with distinguished regards again, Your Most Devoted and Obliged, Giuseppe Sarto, Bishop of Mantua, Secretary of the Conference'.

This stately rhodomontade was sent by Bishop Sarto, later to be a figure of immense importance, to the young Brescian musician and scholar Giovanni Tebaldini (1864-1952), who had given 'theoretical and practical lectures on Sacred Music' on 19 and 20 September 1892, when the Lombardy Region Society of Saint Gregory had been founded in the small town of Vaprio d'Adda, north of Milan. He was a major campaigner on behalf of the Cecilianist cause in the course of a long life, and in the 1890s gave many more such lectures to learned audiences, clerical and otherwise, throughout northern Italy.[102]

Meanwhile, an unusual event had occurred in the Vatican: Mustafà received a letter, dated 18 May, from Angelo Del Nero, who was Italian Special Commissioner for the Department of Fine Arts of the World's Columbian Exhibition, to be held in Chicago the following year. He was inviting the Sistine Choir to perform there, perhaps before the extraordinary assembly, known as the 'Parliament of World Religions', whose meeting at the Exhibition was much trumpeted. The invitation was refused: 'for reasons of delicacy and decorum, and also *per questione d'interesse*'.[103] This is a most revealing phrase, literally meaning 'owing to a matter of interest', words in themselves as bland as 'reasons of delicacy and decorum'; but an alternative and equally valid translation would be 'for reasons of self-interest'.[104] Mustafà may well have feared a palace (or rather 'chapel') coup in the choir's absence, not least since Monsignor Scilla, whom the whole choir regarded as its 'benefactor and reformer',[105] no longer had the Pope's ear as his major-domo, but was now a cardinal.

The distractions of possible international travel notwithstanding, Mustafà, with Moreschi, other soloists, and the entire choir now had a home-grown project to occupy them greatly: the Golden

Jubilee of Pope Leo's consecration to the episcopate. The event was recorded in glowing terms in the Sistine Diary for 19 February 1893: 'At the beginning of the mass the singers of the papal chapel intoned the new chorus "Jubilate Deo" by the most distinguished master Mustafà. The majesty of the music, faithfully interpreted, the marvellous execution which one can hear only from singers of the profession who are Roman, was to an extraordinary degree in harmony with the solemnity of the occasion.' This is certainly self-praise, and there is a lot more mutual 'back-patting' to be found in the Diaries for this year, written by the then *segretario-puntatore* Giovanni Verusio.[106] Were the members of the choir beginning to feel threatened and in need of mutual encouragement? In a letter dated 7 October the new major-domo, Monsignor della Volpe, wrote to Mustafà '. . . with the way the wind is blowing, believe me, Professor, it will be quite an achievement if you succeed in preserving the status quo . . . '

As yet, there was little public sign of any threat to that status quo, but there were more testing times to come. The Sistine's whole tradition of performing Palestrina was soon to receive closer public scrutiny than perhaps ever before. It is remarkable how the course of Moreschi's life was so frequently decided by historical coincidence and consequent events quite beyond his control, but this was certainly another such. The year 1894 saw the tercentenary of the death of Palestrina, and on 26 April of that year a *solenne accademia* was held in the Sala Clementina of the Papal Palace to celebrate this anniversary. It was not a private concert, and critical reception was favourable: 'Mustafà has vied with Palestrina, and has given us an interpretation so new that one might well call it a second creation. Who in Rome has not heard the *Peccavimus*? Nonetheless, yesterday Mustafà drew from the music effects so new that it seemed to all to be a thing never heard before and of a beauty altogether new and rare. On leaving the great hall there was a common feeling that this was the true music of the Church, that this alone is appropriate to the worship of God and his saints.'[107] This report by a journalist from Turin finds echoes in a letter from the Pope to Mustafà himself, but His Holiness's reactions are predictably more subtle. After giving his thanks for the choir's many proofs of 'filial devotion' and praising Mustafà for using his abilities 'to replenish and cherish the famous traditions of the Sistine', he gives a considerable eulogy of the choir's performances at his jubilee, at a memorial service for his parents, and at the Palestrina celebrations. He then continues: 'In better days your College might take up again the splendid role which it always played during the sacred mysteries. Endeavour meanwhile to maintain the assiduous exercise of your usual practice; and let each of you make every effort worthily to maintain decorum. To which end I beg on your behalf the abundance of God's grace, and with paternal affection impart to all, you especially, beloved son, my apostolic blessing.[108] This may seem like unequivocal praise, but the tone of the letter, while typically diplomatic, is somehow not wholeheartedly positive, with a possible implication that the choir 'could try harder'. Leo, though, obviously respected the work and abilities of Mustafà and his choir, and wished for continuity rather than any sudden break with the past.

However, the Holy Father was by this date not only aware of movements for church music reform, having given Franz Xaver Witt an audience as long ago as 1878, but was indeed promoting them. On 6 July 1894 the Congregation of Sacred Rites had added further instructions to its 1884 *Regulations* by issuing the *Normae pro musica sacra* 'with the approval of Leo XIII',[109] which particularly referred to the need to reform church music at a diocesan level within Italy. There is a distinct sense here of forces homing in on what were coming increasingly to be seen as corrupt traditions.

On the other hand, it is not the case that the Cecilianists were the only ones seeking to cleanse the Church's music. Mustafà's frequently-performed edition of Palestrina's motet *Peccavimus* had been issued by the house of Pacifico Manganelli, a well-known Roman publisher of sacred music, as the first of a series entitled 'Periodic Publication of Sacred Music realized under the Auspices of the Sacred Congregation for the Doctrine of the Faith'. Manganelli, in his preface to the first volume writes that because of 'the decadence, and even aberrance of sacred music' it is necessary to print examples of 'the art as it should be'.[110] Printing Mustafà's edition of the Palestrina motet with all his editorial additions as the first in the whole series, and as an example of church music not corrupted, not decadent, and not aberrant, would have made any Cecilianist see red, but, as well as being published with the specific approbation of the Sacred Congregation, the series carried letters of approval from the Pope (via his Latin Secretary) and from Signor Marchetti, President of the Accademia di Santa Cecilia (a separate secular organisation not connected with Cecilianism as such, and now the prestigious national music academy).

It must be remembered that Mustafà's *Peccavimus* edition had appeared as long ago as 1878 (a few months before Pius IX's death) and perceptions of the relative desirability of tradition and reform had clearly been changing in the intervening decade and a half, as Cecilianism gathered strength. Not all their criticism was as subtle as the Pope's had been: Monsignor Grassi Landi, Roman correspondent of the Milanese journal *Musica Sacra,* clearly regarded the Sistine Chapel as a very Augean stable of musical corruption, describing the Choir's rendering of the Credo from Palestrina's *Missa Papae Marcelli* in these terms: ' . . . with the exception of the *Incarnatus* it was, as you might say, sung all of a piece and stupefyingly loud . . . Why from this masterpiece banish all colour? Was it not possible . . . to enhance each part by tempering and moderating such exaggerated loudness?'[111] It is hard to believe that he is writing about the same *accademia* praised in *L'Italia Reale* of Turin [see above pp 102-103], and by the pontiff himself.

The dispute over the merits of the Sistine's work soon developed into something of a critical see-saw. In 1895, Mustafà brought Palestrina's mass *Hodie Christus Natus Est* into the chapel repertoire for the first time, and one Roman newspaper wrote: 'Here it pleases us to repeat what we have already said before, that the Pontifical Chapel adheres strongly to its traditions, with truly irreproachable performances of classical sacred music.'[112] As far as the Cecilianists were concerned, those traditions were the whole problem. Monsignor Grassi Landi returned to the fray – of the choir's performance at the mass for the Anniversary of the death of Pope Pius IX on 7 February 1896 he opined: 'The Mass was performed with less accuracy than on other occasions, even though the very pews knew it off by heart . . .' This was quite enough for the choir-members: the *maestro pro tempore* Cesare Boezi decided to carry the argument back to the very body which was promulgating the reforms under dispute. He wrote an indignant letter of protest to the Prefect of the Sacred Congregation of Rites himself, Andrea Ferrari, Cardinal Archbishop of Milan: 'The levity with which the directors of the periodical *Musica Sacra* . . . prefer to welcome to their columns correspondence with few exceptions unrelated to the truth, and only because it contains denigration of all music performed in Rome, and particularly that by the Pontifical Chapel, drives me to intrude upon Your Eminence, and to distract you from the care of your pastoral ministry. Eminence, pray deign to inspect the various correspondence sent to this periodical from Rome by a self-styled amateur critic of the musical arts on the occasion of . . . the performance given by the pontifical singers for the tercentenary of the death of the Prince of sacred music . . . when there were so many present in Rome of great distinction in the field – not one had anything but words of sincere praise for our most beloved Perpetual Director . . . Concerning this concert, the only strident voice raised against this praise was the false and malign report of the correspondent of the above-named journal, who took no account of the faithful reports of public satisfaction made in all the newspapers . . . ?'[113]

Boezi the professional musician goes on to lambast the Monsignor's amateurishness in misidentifying some of the music performed, and asks, quite reasonably, how he can pretend to criticize performances when he can't even distinguish one composer's works from another's. He gets very heated, referring to Grassi Landi's *spudorate menzogne* ('shameless lies'), and aims a telling blow at *Musica Sacra* by effectively reporting the journal to the Congregation of Sacred Rites for infringing its ban on polemic in the field of sacred music, which he justifiably describes as a 'vain hope'. He also pointedly reminds His Eminence that *Musica Sacra* is published in his own arch-diocese (Tebaldini was, incidentally, a prime mover of this publication), and that the Monsignor, a member of the Chapter of St Peter's Basilica, has his salary paid by the Vatican. The singers were justifiably indignant at sharing the papal pay-roll with one who would destroy them, but Grassi Landi was not to be beaten: '. . . it is certainly not ill-will that makes me write in such a way, but the burning desire that I cherish that the Sistine Chapel might again deserve the fame which it enjoyed through its own merits a century ago . . . I am not the only one to lament the course which the Chapel has taken in recent years with regard to singing. I do not speak of the offertories, post-communion chants and the introits hammered-out and harmonized in octaves, fifths and thirds. . . which reveal nothing of tradition, but rather of the lack of skill in Gregorian chant. Of Palestrina moreover, in these last years, they always perform the same few things . . .'[114] The tendentious nostalgia and sententiousness of his comments is remarkable, and, as Boezi said, the critic gets things wrong: the harmonizing of chant did have a long tradition behind it and only a year before Mustafà had introduced a work by Palestrina into the Sistine repertoire which had never been performed there before.

At the time, part of the fault in this dispute certainly lay with

Mustafà, and for the usual reason: absence. Many of the criticisms that had been directed at the choir were of performances directed by senior members: the castrato Giovanni Cesari, the bass Emilio Calzanera, and of course Pasquali. Had Mustafà been present, he would surely have made protests himself, rather than exposing Boezi to possible censure from above. It took another gentle grumble from His Holiness to bring the Director back '. . . as the major-domo said, the motets sung on 13 April did not succeed in satisfying greatly the ears of His Holiness. The reason for this was in the choice of motets, all for full choir, without soloists, and all by Palestrina. Music in the pure style of Palestrina, profound in its composition, doesn't always satisfy the ears of those who are not professional musicians. This being the case, Boezi, as *maestro pro tempore*, wrote a letter to maestro Mustafà, begging him that if it pleased him, he might return to Rome, because under his able direction it would be possible to perform motets of his own composition . . .'[115]

April the thirteenth that year fell only eight days after Easter, so, extraordinarily enough, Mustafà may have been away during the whole Easter feast. Perhaps he had not yet realised the vulnerability of his position, or thought that the Vatican's historical conservatism would still protect him. Leo was quite happy to reveal that he himself didn't like acres of unsweetened Palestrina, but preferred a little modern music to leaven the mix. Grassi Landi and the Cecilianists would not have been pleased, but for how much longer, in the face of their onslaught, could Mustafà's beloved status quo be sustained by tickling the Pope's ears?

Mustafà certainly came back in quite a hurry, and seems to have at last realised that something had to be done to put things right. On 15 April he had an audience with the Pope, which resulted in the issue of another decretal, a supplement to the *Regolamento* of 1891. This at first appears to be mainly concerned with some fairly minor tinkering with the choir's finances, but also acknowledges at last that only by the fudge of including retired members will the

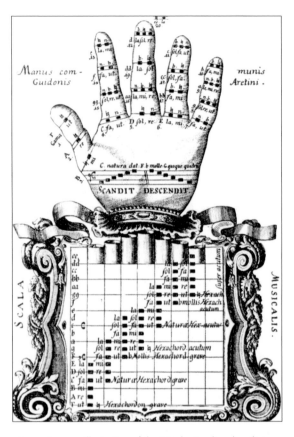

A renaissance illustration of the Guidonian hand outlining
Guido d'Arezzo's system of sol-fa

choir's strength ever return to the officially designated 32: a sad
admission. However, Article Seven is about more than fiddling
with statistics: 'The major-domo's office . . . will make use of the
100 Lire . . . from Article 4 and the 140 Lire . . . from Article 5
to provide the religious, literary and musical education of two
castrated children . . .'[116] How His Holiness and his Perpetual
Director could have conceived of such a retrograde step is unbe-
lievable. Castration of boys 'for the glory of God' had been illegal

for over a quarter of a century, so where these children would have appeared from, and by what means they could have been smuggled into the Sistine Choir, is impossible to conceive. The Pope had never recognised the power of the Italian state, but the scandal that would have erupted had such children been discovered would have been overwhelming. This in a document which begins: 'His Holiness . . . taking into consideration the petition of the Perpetual Director of the College of the singers of the papal Chapel, and intending always to regulate better its moral, economic and physical state . . .' Perhaps Leo was being politically adroit, and merely humouring Mustafà in an old man's nostalgic fantasy, for all that the latter was famous for having once threatened to kill whoever had had him castrated sixty years previously.

What this Article does show is that, to the last, Mustafà was actually far from countenancing change, perhaps because his sixty years of work were beginning to take their toll. Though warmly welcomed back by his colleagues, Mustafà was nearing 70, and realised that he could not continue in the service of the Sistine Chapel indefinitely. He did, however, take the choir to Arezzo in July 1896 to perform at celebrations in honour of the ninth centenary of the birth of the famous music-theorist, Guido d'Arezzo.

Guido d'Arezzo (c990-c1050) was an Italian Benedictine monk and great music theorist, particularly in the field of notation. He developed the system of *sol-fa* for designating musical pitches that, with some modifications, is still used today.

These took place during a Congress on Sacred Music held in the city, which roundly condemned traditional practices in the performance of both polyphony and plainchant: a depressing outcome for Mustafà and his colleagues. He saw the new Papal decree brought into force on 16 November 1897, but on 14 March 1898, he celebrated the 50th anniversary of his admission to the choir, and shortly thereafter decided definitively to retire. He was perhaps helped on his way by further official mutterings. The Pope's new major-domo, Monsignor Francesco Salesio Della Volpe wrote to the *maestro pro tempore* Antonio Comandini that the choir's performance at a funeral mass on 19 September for the recently-assassinated Empress Elizabeth of Austria 'left something to be desired', and though he later excused himself for his 'somewhat exaggerated and over-severe remarks', he once again exhorted the papal singers to be 'more diligent in future'.[117]

This official, posed photograph of the Sistine Chapel choir was taken on 4 March 1898, when the choir would have been celebrating the 30th anniversary of the coronation of Pope Leo XIII (strictly, the day before). As well as showing them in their still very clerical finery, it is probably the largest gathering of castrati ever in one photograpyh: as well as Moreschi (no 16) and Mustafà (no 26), there is also Cesari (no 8), Salvatori (no 15), Sebastianelli (no 18), Pesci (no 29) and Ritarossi (no 30). One can easily see how varying in physique the castrati were, just like 'ordinary' men. None of them looks grotesque or freakish in the least: Cesari and Salvatori are certainly tall, but Sebastianelli is of similar height to Moreschi, who really does seem rather hunched – perhaps osteoporosis, a common problem for castrati, was setting in, although he was only 39 when this photograph was taken.

Winds of Change 1898-1903

With yet another admonishment of 'could do better' ringing in his ears, it is easy to understand why Mustafà might think that enough was enough. All of his three colleagues at the papal basilicas, with whom he had worked more or less harmoniously throughout his career, had died (Capocci as recently as January), so he may have felt somewhat bereft and isolated. It is extraordinary also that there was no-one in Rome whom he thought worthy of his post. However, he did have to consider the weighty question of his successor, and his choice was the very young Lorenzo Perosi, a 26 year-old priest-musician from Tortona in Lombardy. Perosi had achieved early fame as a composer with his *Passion according to St Mark* (1897) and *Resurrection of Christ* (1898), and this was no doubt one means by which Mustafà came to know of his obvious talent. However remarkable it may seem that Mustafà hit upon someone 43 years his junior as a potential 'guardian of the Sistine flame', he clearly hoped and believed that in Perosi he had identified an assistant who 'would be able, under his direction, to maintain and defend the traditions and glories of the Chapel . . .'[118] Despite their identical titles, Mustafà clearly thought of Perosi as his assistant rather than his equal. Whether through vanity or a deep-seated fear of competition, this was to prove to be a source of many difficulties during the next few years.

Perosi was appointed joint Perpetual Director at a papal audience on 15 December 1898, and the following day he wrote to Mustafà: 'it is my most lively desire to continue, with your advice, the fine traditions of the historic Chapel.'[119] The weasel word here is 'historic', and we are again up against the problem of differing perceptions of Sistine tradition. During the 1880s, Don Lorenzo had met Bishop Sarto of Mantua, who had encouraged him to study in Regensburg with Franz Xaver Haberl, a leading German proponent of Cecilianism. He had also visited the monks of Solesmes, and thus become involved with both parties concerned with the revising of the Church's Gregorian chant repertoire. In 1893 Sarto became Patriarch of Venice, where he appointed Perosi Director of the choir of St. Mark's the following year. Perosi also knew Tebaldini well, and so all in all was a man of purest Cecilianist principle.

His idea of 'historic' was therefore very different from that of his aged predecessor, and this soon became clear to Mustafà 'who had been disappointed that he could make of him a perpetuator of the particular methods, by means of which . . . he defined the "true traditions" of the Chapel.'[120] Perosi's appointment was also not popular with the Roman newspapers, who complained about the fact that, for the first time in history, the Sistine Chapel choir would be led by an outsider. From a non-Roman viewpoint, a less incestuous relationship with the Sistine Chapel might have been seen as an advantage.

The singers themselves could not have been at all happy, caught between two directors of equal rank, but widely diverging ideas.[121] Many would have felt sentimentally attached to their old ways, and understandably fearful of what was to come. As was so often the case in the Vatican, however, nothing definite happened for a while. Perosi, still in charge of music at St Mark's, Venice and conducting widely, was rarely in Rome, so Mustafà continued as *de facto* Director for three more years. During this period, however, the fact that Perosi was officially of equal status with him obviously rankled. In 1899, wishing to close his fifty years of service to the Chapel by taking charge of the music at a service in memory of Pius IX on 7 February, and another to mark the anniversary of Leo XIII's coronation on 3 March, he discovered that these duties had been assigned to his young rival. The resulting brouhaha was only resolved (in Mustafà's favour) by the direct intervention of Major-domo Della Volpe. The latter was also on the receiving end of complaints from Mustafà about Perosi's decision to do away with the age-old practice of all the performers reading from one enormous score on a central music-stand, for which Bregno's choir-loft in the Sistine was clearly designed. Here Mustafà seems quite justified in fearing a loss of unanimity and flexibility from his performers.

There was more friction over the ceremony of canonization for Rita of Cascia and John Baptist de la Salle on May 24 1900, when Mustafà threatened to resign unless Perosi let him take charge. He was clearly determined to make the occasion as traditional as possible, since on this day he conducted the Sistine Choir's last ever performance of Gregorian chant with *falsobordone* harmonisation.[123] Their appearance at this ceremony may also provide a solution to one of the many mysteries surrounding Moreschi's career. It has been often remarked that Alessandro's fame as a singer spread beyond Rome, and indeed beyond Italy.[124] One particularly odd tale relates to his having gone to the French city of Lyons to participate in a commemoration of Beethoven there in 1900. Many French pilgrims came to the canonisation of John Baptist de la Salle, and Lyons was a major centre of the educational work done by the Order of Christian Brothers that he had founded. Important

In one sense at least it was on this day that the modern world reached the Vatican. For the first time, 600 Edison carbon electric lamps burned in the Choir of the basilica, and the "glory" at the top of Bernini's Throne of St Peter was lit with electric stars.[125] As there was no general electric lighting in Rome at this date, the Vatican's own engineers constructed a generator producing 24 horsepower.

Brothers would have been present at the ceremony, heard Moreschi, and might have asked him to sing for them. Whether this ever happened, and what possible link to Beethoven (perhaps not an ideally 'Catholic' composer) there may have been remains to be seen, though it is possible that memories of Alessandro's early fame as the Seraph in Beethoven's *Christ on the Mount of Olives* still lingered. In these troubled times Moreschi, concerned to hold on to his means of earning a living, had been careful as long ago as 1896 to obtain official permission to become a full member of the Cappella Giulia and the Lateran choir – covering his back, as it were, but otherwise keeping a low profile.[126] He and his two remaining castrato colleagues, Salvatori and Sebastianelli, would have been acutely aware that any invasion of the Sistine Chapel by the forces of Cecilianism would mean an end to their careers there, since the castrato voice was the epitome of Sistine degeneracy for Tebaldini, Perosi and their ilk.

However, the secular outside world was about to invade the singer's daily life in a most unexpected way, taking his mind off domestic concerns for a time. On 29 July in the northern city of Monza, King Umberto I of Italy was assassinated by the anarchist Gaetano Bresci. Permission for Alessandro to sing at the King's funeral was specially granted by the Pope. Moreschi had already had contact with the Italian royal family, having been a regular soloist at the annual memorial masses for Umberto's father, Vittorio Emmanuele II, who had died in 1878.[127] There is also the possibility of a more direct link, since the King's widow, Queen Margherita, had, like Moreschi, been a pupil of Capocci. The music for the funeral mass, held in the Pantheon on 9 August, was under the direction of the composer Pietro Mascagni (1863-1945, already famous for his opera *Cavalleria Rusticana*). Reports in Italian newspapers of the time seem somewhat confused as to exactly what music was performed at the King's funeral, but there were certainly movements sung from a mass by Palestrina, and music by his near contemporaries Giovanni Anerio (1567-1630) and Tomas Luís de Victoria (1548-1611).[128] The choir of 160 was drawn from conservatoires throughout Italy, and performed hidden from the congregation behind the high altar. Exactly what role Moreschi played is unclear: his participation having been especially requested by the royal family, he would hardly not have performed as a soloist, and the most likely piece for him to have taken part in was the *Libera me* by Eugenio Terziani (1824-1889) – a few years later Moreschi was to record that composer's *Hostias*, with text also from the Requiem Mass.[129] It was indeed amazing that Alessandro was present at the ceremony at all, since relations between the Vatican and the State were still more or less frozen, in spite of a change of monarch and of pope since the unification of Italy. The funeral mass was celebrated by Tommaso Reggio, the elderly Archbishop of Genoa, and there were no official representatives from the Vatican present. It was not least a testimony to Moreschi's continuing public reputation that he was allowed to perform on so important a state occasion.

It has often been written that Moreschi sang at the funerals of two Italian kings. This stems at least partly, from a misinterpretation of the Italian word *funerali*; *funerale* does indeed mean 'funeral', but also has a secondary meaning of 'requiem mass', without the body present. Moreschi was in any case little-known at the time of the death of Umberto's father, Vittorio Emmanuele II, in 1878, and the presence of any Papal singer at that earlier date would have been quite impossible, given the prevailing political situation.

Perosi's seeming deference to Mustafà during this period may be explained by the fact that he knew that time was on his side. The older man had officially decided to retire, and, in any event, the confusion and disruption of having two directors of the Sistine Choir could not go on for ever.

The funerary casket
of King Umberto I
in the Pantheon;
painting by
Adriano Ferraresi

Matters came to a head on 3 February 1902, when Perosi managed, in audience with the 92 year-old pontiff, to obtain a papal injunction forbidding further recruitment of castrati to the Sistine Chapel choir.[130] As long ago as 1888, when he was only 16, Perosi had heard Moreschi singing an aria from Donizetti's *La Favorita*.[131] Whether this led to a lifelong dislike of the castrato voice, or whether it was simply part-and-parcel of his modernising Cecilianist viewpoint, is hard to say.

It is no surprise that Mustafà attempted to have the injunction overturned, but without success. Remarking 'that above all, if the established abuse of admitting young singers from other Roman choirs into the Sistine Chapel be retained, they, by their method of singing, will bring about the loss of [its] historic traditions . . .' he tendered his resignation once more.[132] This time, though, his bluff was called, and the Pope accepted it, subtly re-naming him 'Honorary Perpetual Director'.

Mustafà's final appearance as conductor of the choir was not a happy one. At the 24th anniversary of the Pope's coronation on 4 February 1902, the choir 'did not show itself to be up to the level of its task'.[133] 'The abiding problem of the singers of the Sistine Chapel is now being studied by the Pope's Major-domo, Monsignor Cagiano de Azevedo . . . The poor performance given by the singers of the Sistine Chapel on the day of the Pope's jubilee . . . is likely to have furnished an excuse for further consideration of proposals for reform, which had previously been laid to rest for several months. . . Mustafà, Director of the Sistine laid down as a condition of his retirement not only the retention of the present *voci bianche*, but also that the organisation of the Sistine Chapel be preserved in every detail . . .' The reforms in question had, of course, been formulated by Perosi: 'by which the present sopranos will be replaced by young Palestrinian singers . . . '[134] Probably realising that he had presided over a below par performance, and in the hope of applying pressure, Mustafà made the mistake of telling the newspapers, as well as His

Holiness, that he was going to resign – that no doubt annoyed the Pope enormously, and provided another pretext for the resignation to be accepted.

In the midst of such upheaval, the one event that made Moreschi famous, rather than merely a footnote to a footnote in the history of singing and Catholic church music, occurred, and once again, occurred by coincidence. In this case it involved the earliest commercial history of recorded sound. In 1897, William Barry Owen, a director of Émil Berliner's National Gramophone Company in Washington, had moved to London to set up a European branch named The Gramophone Company. In 1900 this had become The Gramophone and Typewriter Company, of which he was Managing Director. On 11 March 1902 he was in Milan, and heard the as yet not world-famous Enrico Caruso's sensational performance in the premiere of Alberto Franchetti's opera *Germania* at La Scala. Owen instructed Alfred Michaelis, Director of his Milan office, to record Caruso, sending over their head 'recordist' in London, the American recording engineer Fred Gaisberg.[135] Discovering that Caruso was unavailable for an encounter with Gaisberg's machinery for several days, he and Michaelis travelled to Rome, where the latter had already

Fred Gaisberg (1873-1951) was one of the most important figures during the first half-century of recording history, both as a recording engineer and talent scout. Early in his career he was also a piano accompanist for vocal recordings, and became the friend of many great singers, including Caruso and Melba. He discovered the superiority of shellac over the previously used hard rubber for the manufacture of discs and was also the first to understand the importance of a clock-work mechanism in obtaining accurate playback speed.

attempted to negotiate recording the voice of the Pope himself. Leo, who preferred to rely in such matters on faith rather than technology, had already turned down this perhaps dubious opportunity for

A photograph of Fred Gaisberg, seen here with Sir Edward Elgar and Yehudi Menuhin outside the Abbey Road Studios in London in 1932

auditory immortality the year before.[136] Gaisberg was keen to promote the still very new medium of the gramophone record through recording famous artists, and would therefore have been open to the unique opportunity presented by Moreschi and the Sistine Choir.

Through Michaelis's Vatican contacts, he would no doubt have heard that it was likely that the castrati were soon to disappear for good. He wrote in his diaries: ' . . . instead of setting up our recording apparatus in a mere hotel, we were directed to the palace of the Vatican. Selecting a great salon with walls covered with Titians, Raphaels and Tintorettos, we mounted our grimy machine right in the middle of the floor, attached three trumpets or collecting horns and waited. . . . Michaelis, through his friend Captain Pecci of the Swiss bodyguard, the Pope's nephew, had involved himself in a tangle of complicated wire-pulling, the result of which was the acquisition of records of the famous Sistina Cap[p]ella . . . and perhaps the voice of the Pope . . . himself . . . [the choir] was noted for preserving the music of Palestrina and for the beauty of its singing, due to the male sopranos, which dispensed with boy sopranos, thus adding to the solidity of the singing. The practice of obtaining male sopranos for the choir was discontinued after Leo XIII, and those who formed our choir were simply carefully selected males with natural soprano and alto voices . . . I particularly remember their rosy-cheeked conductor[137] and solo soprano, Professor Moreschi, whom I then judged to be about sixty but who was amazingly fresh and youthful and boasted of a large family, which greatly interested me.'[138]

To put it mildly, this last sentence is something of a surprise, though of course, 'family' need not refer to children of his own – Moreschi had several siblings, and presumably a whole tribe of nephews and nieces by then. However, Gaisberg does seem to have edited his diaries for publication, maybe fearing squeamish reaction. His original text stated: ' . . . we made records of the Sistine Cap[p]ella, the celebrated male choir of the Pope . . . the soprano voice parts are all sung by men who have been operated on in their youth.'[139] Perhaps Moreschi himself was also embarrassed about his physical state in front of someone who had no knowledge of Sistine tradition or the castrato voice. Gaisberg also considerably overestimates Moreschi's age: he was only 43 at the time. A castrato's facial skin remained fine and beardless throughout his life, but often developed fine wrinkles as he aged, which may have confused Gaisberg.

In this session seven recordings were made,[140] in all of which Moreschi can be heard as either a soloist or member of an ensemble. Other than the significance of these as a unique record of the sound of the castrato voice, the whole situation is a fascinating comment on internal Vatican politics at that time. It is clear that Pope Leo knew that the recordings were happening and had sanctioned them – there are several 'great salons' in the Vatican, most within earshot of the Papal Apartments. All of the sacred music recorded is of the neo-theatrical school, whether by contemporary composers or, horror of horrors, Mozart, and thus of that type so much disliked by the Cecilianists. Since it was therefore in imminent danger of being permanently removed from the repertoire, perhaps it was not only the singers in the Vatican who saw the value of recording it for posterity.

These recording sessions took place between 3 and 5 April (Gaisberg returned to Milan to record Caruso on 11 April). It is likely that they happened without the knowledge of Perosi, who by this time had grown obsessive about castrati, equating them, quite unjustifiably, with people of mental and sexual instability. He felt that his desire to remove castrati from the Sistine Chapel choir needed public justification: 'The substitution [of boys for castrati] has cost me more mental strain than all the music I have composed. But I insisted on it for a grave moral reason, since, shortly after my arrival in Rome, so many requests to join the choir began reaching me from abnormal men that I suspected some ignoble speculation behind them, particularly as some of these unfortunate youngsters presented themselves to me in person.'[141] Whoever these so-called 'abnormal men' were, they were certainly not castrati! All that being said, he certainly respected Mustafà as a musician, and valued the friendship of Moreschi and his colleague Sebastianelli. However keenly he advocated reform, Perosi was a complicated man of ambiguous attitudes.

On the professional front his will prevailed at last. As well as reporting his worries about the perils of recruiting suitable singers, the same 28 December issue of the Rome newspaper *La Tribuna* reported: 'A decision "ex audientia sanctissima", taken some months ago and kept secret until now, has just been transformed into a decree and will come into operation at once: as a result those singers who, let us say, are "imperfect" on a physical plane although . . . complete as singers, are totally excluded from the Sistine Chapel. This constitutes a victory for Maestro Perosi who had suggested this reform ever since he entered the Sistine . . . In any case, this recent decree means that the famous inscription which could be read barely a century ago outside a barber's shop in the Banchi Vecchi, "Boys castrated here for the Papal Chapel", now becomes an . . . archaeological memory.'[142]

Mustafà's final leave-taking was also carried out publicly. *La Vera Roma* for 25 January 1903 published a letter to him from the choir: 'Illustrious and Honoured Master, It is with the liveliest and deepest regret that we . . . have learned of your irrevocable decision to leave your post as our Perpetual Director . . . We who for a period of 55 years have had you as our leader and master in the sublime art of singing . . . cannot hold back from . . . expressing the most bitter sorrow that we feel at our separation from you . . .' Mustafà's response also appeared: 'I must confess to you likewise that not without piercing thorns have I had to stifle in my heart my dearest wish: to be able to close my eyes on life and art in your midst . . . you who in your goodness have tolerated me to the utmost . . .' Effusive this may seem, but both sides also spoke warmly of Perosi and his abilities. Public dignity was maintained, whatever private griefs and misgivings may have been felt.

Such worries were apparently not unjustified. On 7 February, the 25th anniversary of the death of Pius IX, Perosi made his first appearance as sole Perpetual Director, conducting the *Requiem* by Palestrina's contemporary Felice Anerio: 'the debut was not good . . . several people noticed the lack of emotional effects and an evident disorientation on the part of the singers, who performed their role lifelessly and with uncertain intonation.'[143] Whether this was deliberate on the singers' part, or, more likely, the understandable result of being 'under new management' is hard to say. What is certain is that the final departure of Mustafà heralded the end of an era, and a tradition, almost 350 years old.

A Long Twilight

A few months after Mustafà's sad final departure for his home-town of Montefalco, Pope Leo XIII died, aged 93. On 31 July the College of Cardinals met in Conclave to elect his successor. Since the fall of the Papal States in 1870, the voting in the Conclave had taken place in the Sistine Chapel. After five rather sensational days involving the imposition of the Emperor of Austria's veto against one candidate, and rumours of the attempted poisoning of several cardinals during their sequestration, a successful candidate was elected by a large majority. Thus, on 4 August 1903, the final triumph of Cecilianism was assured, since the new pope, who had taken the name Pius X, was none other than Giuseppe Melchiorre Sarto, former Bishop of Mantua and Patriarch of Venice, who had supported that cause for many years. Long before, as a young parish-priest in Salzano, north-west of Venice (1867-1875), he had introduced congregational singing of Gregorian chant, and when Bishop of Mantua had been responsible for setting Perosi on the true Cecilianist path. While Patriarch of Venice, he was zealous in the cause of reform, and made an important deposition to the Sacred Congregation of Rites during the deliberations, which resulted in their 1894 *Normae pro musica sacra* (he had been greatly influenced in this by Father de Santi). Paragraph 13 of a pastoral letter he wrote on 1 May 1895 shows that he would allow nothing to stand in the way of liturgical renewal: 'No account shall be taken of the complaints of singers who will feel themselves aggrieved in that these regulations may

deprive them of their only means of earning a livelihood . . .'[144]
So much for Christian charity.

Despite his new Director's dislike of the castrato voice, Moreschi was probably still singing with the Sistine choir when, as part of its official duties, it sang the motet *Ecce sacerdos magnus* ('Behold the great High Priest') and a *Te Deum* (both presumably by Palestrina), as the assembled Cardinals rendered homage to their new pontiff on August 4. (He is listed in the *Annuario Pontificio* ('Pontifical Yearbook') as a member of the choir until his official retirement in 1913.) Alessandro may justifiably have sung both pieces through clenched teeth. He certainly remained as a member of the Cappella Giulia, and as such he would have sung at the Pope's coronation on 9 August, when, at the Papal blessing, he would have had the galling experience of performing in Palestrina's *Tu es petrus* ('Thou art Peter, the rock on which I shall build my Church'). This particular rock was about to crush Moreschi's career.

Unlike his predecessor, Pius was a northern outsider from a poor family, and also unlike Leo, he was not one to proceed little by little, clearly seeing 'restoration' as an important part of his pontifical ministry. His first encyclical, *E supreme apostolatus cathedra* ('From the Supreme Apostolic Throne') dated 4 October 1903, was subtitled 'On the Restoration of All Things in Christ', and its text hinted that there was a certain need in the Church as a whole for a new broom, while reminding the prelates whom he addressed of 'the tears and earnestness with which We exerted Ourselves to ward off this formidable burden of the Pontificate'. In other words, 'having forced this election upon me, you must now take the consequences.'

The putting of the Church's music back on track was clearly high on his list of priorities, since his next missive was the *motu proprio*, *Tra le Sollecitudini* ('Amongst the Cares'), which appeared, appropriately enough, on St Cecilia's day, 22 November (a *motu proprio* is a type of papal rescript issued on the Pope's personal initiative). This was the final nail in the coffin of all that Mustafà, Moreschi and their colleagues stood for, remarking as it did on 'the fatal influence exercised on sacred art by profane and theatrical art. 'The ancient tradition of the Gregorian Chant must . . . be restored . . . classic polyphony agrees admirably with the Gregorian Chant, the supreme model of all sacred music, and hence it has been found worthy of a place side by side with the Gregorian chant in the more solemn functions of the Church, such as those of the pontifical Chapel . . . modern music has risen mainly to serve profane uses . . . What appears less suitable for accompanying the forms of public worship is the theatrical style . . . the music rendered by them [singers in church] must, at least for the greater part, retain the character of choral music . . . solo singing should never predominate . . . Whenever . . . it is desirable to employ the high voices of sopranos and contraltos, these parts must be taken by boys, according to the most ancient usage of the Church. . . . '

The Pope followed this up with specific instructions concerning the churches of Rome, which were under the control of his Vicar-General, Cardinal Pietro Respighi, who had himself long been a supporter of the reforms in question. On 8 December 1903, the feast of the Immaculate Conception, Pius wrote that 'the beautiful musical traditions of the classical Roman school are no longer to be found. For the devout psalmody of the clergy, in which the people also used to join, there have been substituted interminable musical compositions on the words of the psalms, all of them modelled on old theatrical works and most of them of such meagre artistic value that they would not be tolerated for a moment even in our second-rate concerts. It is certain that Christian piety and devotion are not promoted by them; the curiosity of some of the less intelligent is fed, but the majority, disgusted and scandalized, wonder how it is that such an abuse can still survive. We therefore wish the cause to be completely extirpated. . . the patriarchal basilicas will lead the way . . . And you, My Lord Cardinal, must neither accept excuses nor concede delays . . . ' He also mentioned ' . . . the want of capacity and the imperfect taste of the persons to whom the teaching of chant and the direction of sacred music is entrusted . . .'[145] On 8 January 1904, he further reinforced these instructions by issuing a decree forbidding any further performance of music 'in modern forms' in all the major basilicas, 'especially the Lateran', permitting 'no exceptions whatsoever . . .'

Pius had already requested that Cardinal Respighi urge the young clerics of Rome's seminaries to great efforts in learning Gregorian chant, so that they may be ready to join him in the commemoration of the 13th centenary of the death of Pope Gregory the Great, which culminated, after a three-day Congress of academic and monastic scholars and musicians, in a Pontifical High Mass sung in St Peter's on 11 April 1904.[146] The Pope was clearly keen to use all means to disseminate the new edition of Gregorian chant, and invited the Gramophone Company, in the person of William Sinkler Darby, an associate of Gaisberg, back to Rome to record selections of the music performed then. It would appear, however, that His Holiness was not only interested in promoting music in the reformed style. According to Franz Haböck, Darby's discs were made: 'following the intentions of Pope Pius X . . . on the one hand to preserve the achievements of liturgical music, and on the other to create models for the then aimed for reform of church music'.[147] Thus Moreschi and his colleagues were able to make further recordings of the now banned 'pre-*motu proprio*' music. They were clearly not in total disgrace, since Pius (and Perosi) had also permitted them to take part in the mass on 11 April – three castrati were obviously not too much of a pollutant in a choir of 1200.

The recordings made of modernising elements such as speeches from Congress participants and the earliest known discs of the newly-authorised Solesmes versions of chant, (not to mention fanfares played at papal services) have been largely forgotten, but those involving Moreschi and other Sistine singers give a fascinating glimpse into a truly vanished world. Moreschi even made a political point when recording his one disc of plainchant: he used the discarded and strictly illegal Medici edition, as well as all the strange but traditional technical trappings of his twenty-year Sistine experience. It is also surely not by accident that, out of all the thousands of chants available, he sang the opening of the Lamentations of Jeremiah: not in the least bit florid, but perhaps rather making a textual point. There were, though, commercial reasons behind the recording of this and Victoria's *Improperia* since both were well-known to the public, being part of the repertoire for the Holy Week liturgy, which had always remained open to the public, even in the dark days of the 1870s. As to the purities of Palestrina, the only piece in which Moreschi was certainly involved was a madrigal, the text of which begins 'My cruel enemy' – this may just be an ironic coincidence. One wonders whether Pius ever discovered exactly what his singers were getting up to, since, Haböck's remarks notwithstanding, he would at least have gritted his pontifical teeth at the old-style theatrical repertoire they indulged in, even if for the last time.

Darby, though in a difficult position between Moreschi's old guard, Congress participants, and Perosi (who conducted some suitably Cecilianist repertoire for him), handled the situation very well. Careful timetabling to avoid awkward collisions in corridors and saloons between castrati carrying sheets of 'illegal' music, conference delegates with their heads full of neumes, and the volatile Perosi himself would have been necessary. Probably assisted by scurrying Vatican servants used to delicate diplomacy, Darby successfully managed to keep their recording sessions separate, as is shown by the respective matrix numbers of the discs. He was particularly careful with the extract from the Lamentations: its matrix number, the only one of these recordings in the 52000 range, indicates that it was released just for export, and then only to Russia and countries of Eastern Europe – it became extremely rare in the West, but survived safely hidden in realms of Orthodoxy (and Communism).[148]

Moreschi's older colleagues Vissani and Cesari both seem to have died at about this time, but the other remaining Sistine castrati, Sebastianelli and Salvatori, joined Alessandro at the Cappella Giulia of St Peter's basilica(of the other castrati, Pecci was alive, but had already retired, while Ritarossi had died in 1902). The conductor of this Cappella was now Andrea Meluzzi (son of Salvatore), but in January 1905 he was succeeded for a brief while by none other than Moreschi's old colleague from concert party days, Filippo Mattoni. The long-term replacement, from 2 July 1905, was Ernesto Boezi (1856-1947), brother of Moreschi's former tenor colleague Cesare Boezi, who was in some ways almost as much of an anomaly in the new Vatican as were the castrati themselves. He had a background in the secular theatre, having himself written a one-act opera *Don Paez*, premiered at the Teatro la Fenice in Venice in 1893, and been chorus master at the renowned Rome opera theatre, the Teatro Apollo. Here at least was someone with whom Moreschi could feel musically at home – one can imagine him reliving past glories by singing opera arias in the privacy of Boezi's home, while no doubt thoroughly scandalising the neighbours.

Early in November, Moreschi took a brief holiday, on returning from which he made the acquaintance of a talented boy soprano, Domenico Mancini, whose vocal abilities have given rise to some strange stories to the effect that he, rather than Moreschi, was the true 'Last Castrato', and also that he was hidden away in the Vatican so that successive pontiffs could luxuriate in the 'immoral' sound of the castrato voice as late as 1959. To dispel these illusions once and for all, I can do no better than to reproduce Mancini's own words: 'As I had a good voice from a rather young age, I sang in my own church [and] in the cathedral of Civitacastellana. An aunt who came from Rome in the holidays said "this nephew of mine's got such a lovely voice – he'll have to be trained", so she went to Mass at St Peter's, and . . . approached Moreschi because they knew each other . . . An appointment was made, Moreschi listened to me, and told me that, after some preparatory work with him, he would take me along to Maestro Perosi's school. I came to Rome on 14 November 1904, and on the 17th, Moreschi having come back from his vacation (as the 18th was the Feast of the Dedication of St Peter's), another appointment was made, during which he listened to me again and subsequently began to give me lessons. And what superlative lessons they were! He always sang, and I had to imitate him. It was wonderful: I came under the spell of his outstandingly beautiful voice . . . I began my studies with Moreschi by imitating his voice with my own, since, as it hadn't yet changed, I just sang as he did, in chest voice, passing from there into head voice. But then, at around fourteen, well, my voice became that of a man, and so, singing with the falsettists, I began to use the type of head voice which normal adult men have; naturally to sing with it you have to train it, because it's a voice that is made by training and musicianship: you need to be a musician to use it. . . Because I had studied with Moreschi, Perosi thought I was a castrato and didn't want me, since he had rooted out the castrato voices from all the choirs. Those who were there already were kept on until they finished – until their pensions were due. But if there were young ones, they weren't taken on and Perosi got it into his head, since I sang in Moreschi's way, that I was one of 'those' voices. [Instead of to Perosi's school] . . . Moreschi put me to San Salvatore in Lauro, where I . . . went back to elementary school (which I hadn't finished) and then to the Conservatory, to study the double-bass.'[149] Photographs of Mancini in later life also make it clear that he was no castrato, and both his speaking voice and his singing show that he was a moderately skilful falsettist with a perfectly ordinary speaking range.[150] As a falsettist, he sang in the

Domenico Mancini c 1956

Sistine Choir from 1939 to 1959. It is interesting that apparently he could 'fool' Perosi,[151] although the new Director's rejection of him may, I think, have had more to do with not wishing anyone of the old school, like Moreschi, to have any input into the new Sistine environment. Even here, though, there was room for ambiguity: Salvatori, Moreschi's much less prestigious colleague, stayed on at the Sistine, both singing contralto and acting as Choir Secretary to Perosi 'to whom he was most dear, notwithstanding his own aversion to castrati'.[156] Perosi was a man of strong, perhaps even bigoted, principle, but was typically human in not seeing the discontinuity or even hypocrisy between his firmly held dislike of an idea and his friendship for an individual. His friendliness with Salvatori belies his remarks likening castrati to 'abnormal men'.

Pope Pius's *motu proprio* came into full force on 22 June 1905. A sample of Moreschi's singing and that of his colleagues of the old tradition had escaped its strictures, but now, wherever they might see out what remained of their careers, they would be restricted to a repertoire of Palestrina and his contemporaries, and a radically cleaned-up version of chant, both shorn of any

Moreschi in the first decade of the 20th-century

ornament or other means for personal vocal display (official wrangling over chant performance continued throughout the reign of Pius X and beyond). The radically different sound of boy sopranos replaced almost entirely the piercing brilliance of the castrati. Perosi was triumphant, but did not long enjoy his success unalloyed: by 1907 his rather obsessive nature was manifesting itself neurologically, leading to hand tremors which adversely affected his conducting. At a later stage, Perosi's mental state deteriorated severely: he devised an alternative Order for the Mass, modernising the Latin spelling, removing all references to the Trinity, the Lamb of God, the Virgin Mary and the saints, and terming the wine of the communion 'unworthy of God'. He preferred water.[153]

Little is known of the final years of Moreschi's career. Around Easter 1911, he took part in a festival concert at Tivoli, just outside Rome, on the occasion of an International Music Congress, performing choral works by Giovanni Maria Nanino (1545-1607), a pupil of Palestrina. In 1912, Mustafà at last died, after an unhappy retirement blighted by blindness and ill-health. Although Moreschi and some of his colleagues are known to have visited their former Director during his last years, none of them attended his funeral. This may have been because, at this time, there was no Major-domo to the Pope to officially represent the Vatican, or perhaps it was made clear that authorities would not have approved of any pilgrimage on the singers' part.

On 22 March, Easter Saturday 1913, Moreschi completed his thirty-year contract under the Sistine Chapel's regulations, and so qualified for his pension. However, he was still singing in the Cappella Giulia the next year, when, just three months before the outbreak of the First World War, he was interviewed by a visiting Viennese scholar Franz Haböck, a professor of singing at the Academy for Music and Theatre Arts, who had dreams of promoting him on a concert tour of music written for Moreschi's great predecessor Farinelli. Alessandro's range in his youth had been about two and a half octaves, but by this date, according to Haböck, it had shrunk to less than two losing notes and security of emission, particularly at the top. Farinelli's music, which, as well as being often of an extreme floridity which Moreschi had never been trained to encompass, required an enormous range of over three octaves, and would thus have been far beyond his powers. Haböck visited Moreschi during research for his monumental book *Die Gesangskunst der Kastraten*, published in two volumes in Vienna in 1923, and still a classic. He likened the singer's speaking voice to that of a high, rather metallic-sounding tenor, and though noting a certain decline in his vocal powers (Moreschi was then 55) remarked: 'all my informants agreed that Moreschi's voice in its heyday had been of a beauty and strength that they had never heard in a male or female voice. However, he had never possessed the true flexibility of coloratura singing and lacked a trill.[154] On the other hand, his *messa di voce* [art of swelling and dying on a single note] had never been equalled . . . When one wishes to describe the sensual impression a voice makes, one might well say that it has a golden or silver sound, that it feels warm or cold. Moreschi's voice can only be likened to the clarity and purity of crystal. The absolute evenness and timbral unity of his sound, its unusually powerful, clear, transparent and sweet tone, completely different from a woman's or boy's voice, the complete effortlessness, with which, because of his apparently inexhaustible supply of air, one almost physically empathises – all awoke in me a compelling impression of the most beautiful wind instrument ever given life by human breath. . . . When his voice rose above the choir in a crescendo, it overpowered the accompanying boy sopranos as completely as a searchlight outshines a little candle.'[155] It needs remembering that Haböck never heard Moreschi before 1911. In 1914 he comments that the singer's voice was only completely secure in its middle range, so the above glowing account does not describe Alessandro in his prime. Haböck also mentions Christmas madrigal concerts given in Rome hotels during the early years of the 20th-century by members of the Sistine Choir, which may have involved Moreschi, and not particularly successful concert tours to Austria and Germany, which probably didn't: apparently they did not include 'the best singers'.

A last public glimpse of Moreschi is provided by the memoirs of the great Roman tenor Giacomo Lauri-Volpi: 'I came upon the sixty-year-old Moreschi in Via Belsiana [between the Corso and Piazza di Spagna] . . . people turned to look at him. And I heard someone who said "That's Moreschi". He was an ordinary-looking man, of small stature, his lips open in a charming smile. He would have seemed but one among many, had his beardless face not declared something that, given the profession he practised at the Sistine Chapel, recalled those curious anomalies who for two centuries had produced voices of unheard beauty.[156]

The scene described would have taken place in about 1918, and one wonders why Signor Lauri-Volpi didn't speak to the older singer; after all, Giacomo had been a pupil of Moreschi's old colleague and friend Cotogni. They would have had much to talk about, but what may have lain behind Alessandro's 'charming smile', perhaps best lies hidden. Another colleague of his had once remarked enigmatically . . . ' his private life and his relationships were not happy.'[157]

One might also hope that his financial situation was never precarious, since some of his successors at the Sistine Chapel felt a need to make a public protest. On 25 January 1919, five of them published a signed 'Memorandum presented by the Papal Singers to the Most Reverend Canons of the Sistine Chapel', in which they detail long-standing complaints about their pay and conditions. They name the Papal Chamberlain, Monsignor Talamo, as a special problem, stating that he has been suppressing pension rights since 1904. Clearly, some things at the Sistine, Perosian reforms notwithstanding, never changed, as the singers also quote the Monsignor's response, which must have seemed libellous: 'The Papal singers are a bunch of rogues . . . What do they expect? They give the worst possible service and demand a pay-rise. It would be better to abolish them altogether.'[158] Alessandro was clearly well out of this maelstrom.

Around Easter 1919, Moreschi fell prey to an unidentified chronic illness - this is the last year in which he is listed in the *Annuario Pontificio* as an 'emeritus' member of the Sistine Choir. It was at about this time that he truly became 'the Last Castrato', since his former colleague Sebastianelli died on 12 March.

For many years Moreschi had lived in an apartment at Number 19, Via Plinio,[159] in the more modern area of the *rione* Borgo, since renamed Prati, behind the great fortress of Castel Sant'Angelo (the too-prosaic English equivalent of *rione* is 'district': the French word *quartier* is better). This area was one of recent development, with many late 19th-century apartment-blocks, and his address was only a few minutes' stroll from the famous Portone di Bronzo, the main entrance to the Vatican, or the side-door, the Porta Santa Anna, through one of which he had walked more or less every day for thirty years. It was in this apartment that he died, on the morning of 21 April 1922. He had lived through times of struggle between Church and State, between tradition and innovation, through the 'War to end all War' (which ended on his 60th birthday) and to the rise of Italian Fascism.

Though Moreschi's private life may not have been of the happiest, members of his family were with him at the last: 'Today, at nine o'clock in the morning, after a long illness, and supported by Christian resignation, ended with the Lord's kiss the adored life of Professor Alessandro Moreschi, Papal Singer. Amerigo, Giulio and all his relatives, in deepest sorrow, give sad notice of this.'[160] The two named relatives were probably nephews, and it is notable that Moreschi clearly still had many friends, for though his retirement may have been quiet, he had not been forgotten. Three days after the death-notice Alessandro's relatives placed the following in the same newspaper: 'The FAMILY of the lamented Professor Alessandro Moreschi thank all those who wished, with spontaneous displays of affection, to render homage to the memory of their dear departed'. The hearse had left Moreschi's home at 10.30 on the morning of 23 April, and he had clearly been accompanied on his final journey by some former Vatican colleagues and other friends from his musical past.

Moreschi's burial was therefore hardly a private affair, and his requiem mass was certainly public, having been held in an enormous church situated in the Cancelleria, at the heart of Rome's old city. It also gave rise to an extraordinary turn of events: 'One of the artists of sacred music for whom Don Lorenzo Perosi had most regard and affection was Alessandro Moreschi, a fine and noble musician, who had died a few days before. Because of the great friendship which bound them together, the Maestro expressed a wish to conduct the mass for the repose of his soul [which took place] yesterday morning in San Lorenzo in Damaso, with the participation of the finest singers of all the chapels of Rome.'[161] That Perosi, years after his successful removal of the castrati from the Sistine Chapel, should wish to render personal homage to Moreschi in this way is altogether remarkable, particularly since this was at a time when his long-term mental problems were becoming worse and worse. The above remarks are taken from a long article detailing his desire to renounce Catholicism and become a Protestant, and other Italian newspapers were full of lurid reports of his growing insanity.[162] Shortly afterwards Perosi's family had him committed to an asylum. Though he was sufficiently recovered to resume his duties the following year, as the well-worn phrase has it, he was 'never the same again'.

Friends, family and former enemies may have remembered

Moreschi, but Vatican officialdom did not: no notice of his death appeared in the Vatican newspaper *L'Osservatore Romano* nor in the official yearbook, the *Annuario Pontificio*. Whether this was by accident or design is hard to say. Curiously the singer's death-certificate also seems to have disappeared, so perhaps both sacred and secular officialdom found the survival of the last castrato something of an embarrassment. Male sopranos and macho Fascism hardly seem compatible, though the Fascist regime was still young in 1922, and its power and attitudes were by no means all-pervasive.

Fortunately for posterity, Moreschi's singing had already been placed beyond the reach of black-shirt swagger and Vatican fidgeting alike. Another permanent monument, in the shape of his tomb, also survived. In the vastness of the Cimitero del Verano,[163] beyond Rome's huge Termini station, it takes a little finding, but it is worth the search to have a last tangible link with a man whose eerily beautiful voice carries the echoes of centuries.

The tomb of Alessandro Moreschi

The Voice and the Legacy

In chronicling Moreschi's life and times I have purposefully so far kept from discussing his voice and his singing, since, unlike the details of his life, these have already enjoyed considerable public exposure for a number of years. Though so well-known in Rome and beyond during his own lifetime, it is likely that Moreschi will always remain more famous for what he was than for who he was, and we are lucky that, as 'the Last Castrato', his singing was recorded in a permanent form. It is also no enviable task to write about Moreschi's (or any other) singing in a cogent way without the reader's having recordings to hand, and without falling into undue technicality or, worse still, vagueness.

The human vocal instrument consists of the larynx suspended in the throat in an intricate cradle of muscle, ligament and bone, which is acted upon by the breath as it issues from the lungs. In itself, the breath moving across the rapidly opening and closing larynx makes a sound rather like a 'pitched raspberry', blown between tongue and lips, and not a loud one: the resonating chambers of the throat (pharynx) and mouth, plus the resonance of bone-conduction felt in the chest and head, are responsible for converting this unpromising noise into human speech and singing. All adult voices have two mechanisms, called by laryngologists 'modal' ('speaking', in which the vocal cords vibrate together along their entire length) and 'falsetto' (in which, by the action of various cartilages in the throat, the voice 'flips up', as it also does in yodelling; in this mechanism the cords never close entirely, and undeveloped falsetto is very breathy in timbre). These mechanisms, also termed registers, do not operate in exactly the same way for men and women, though even this is a matter of dispute amongst those who write and have written about singing.

The castrato voice was, unsurprisingly, a special case. The vocal cords remained at a pre-pubertal length, similar to those of an adult woman (around half an inch or 12 millimetres). The castrato's larynx was also relatively higher than in the 'normal' adult male, which probably accounts for the shallower timbre of Moreschi's chest register compared to an 'ordinary' tenor. Without the usual male vocal tract development there was also no 'Adam's apple', but this was perhaps the least of the extrinsic differences. Because of the phenomenon of late epiphyseal closure the rib-bones of a castrato remained very flexible when those of other boys were hardening during puberty, and would have been capable of long-continued growth (the epiphyses of the ribs are at the junction with the spine).

The concomitant greater than normal flexibility of the rib-cage at a time when the young castrato was undergoing a period of intensive training may help to account for the castrati's legendary breath capacity, and have given rise to the barrel-chested appearance of castrati frequently seen in 18th-century cartoons.

However, it should be pointed out that castration can also cause the sternum to be short, on the female pattern, and the thoracic volume to be likewise smaller, in

A cartoon of the famous castrato Antonio Bernacchi (1685-1756)

which case flexibility of the chest would be more important than size. (There is a famous breathing exercise, supposedly used by the great Farinelli, which involves slow inflation and deflation of the lungs over for as long as half-a-minute.) As with all human growth patterns, these skeletal phenomena were variable. They do not appear to an exaggerated extent in Moreschi's case, although he does seem to have suffered from another consequence of a castrato's lack of testosterone, namely osteoporosis. By the time of the recordings, especially those of 1904, the slow and late hardening of the ends of his bones was also beginning to have a stiffening effect on his laryngeal cartilages and hyoid bone (from which the larynx is suspended), leading to a gradual lowering of his range. There were many historical precedents for this, and it was not caused by vocal abuse, though it could lead to vocal difficulties, especially in repertoire requiring great flexibility. Some castrati bucked this trend: the famous Gaetano Guadagni discovered his high voice in his middle years and changed from contralto to soprano.

For anyone recording in the first decade of the 20th century, the sheer physical difficulties were considerable, deriving directly from the technological shortcomings of the still new equipment. These are in turn related to the fact that, loud though it can certainly be to the ear, the human voice actually produces very little physical power (as against decibels): a shout registers about one-thousandth of a watt. It was difficult in the early days of recording to devise means of transmitting this tiny amount of power so as to energise the recording diaphragm and cutting stylus of the early wax-cylinder machines. The recording horn, in front of which the singer would need to place and keep his mouth at all times, could also only respond to the limited range of pitches between 165 and 2100 cycles per second. Dynamic effects were only possible by moving the head towards and away from the horn, which didn't exactly help the singer's technique, as Moreschi's pupil Mancini remarked: 'None of us can know the effect of our own voices have, . . . so I made a record as a memoir of . . . a past age. But it's not representative . . . the antics I had to perform to record . . . brought about an alteration even in the intonation.'[164] The limited pitch sensitivity of the early apparatus compares poorly to the full gamut of audible 'live' sound, which ranges from about 20 to 20000 cycles per second, and partly explains why, for example, sopranos recorded at this time can sound thin and tinny. Although the pitches of the human singing voice at its most extreme fall between about 55 and 1760 cycles, this does not include the harmonics of those pitches which add much richness and character to the voice's timbre in the area around 3000 cycles (situated 'at the top of the piano', this is the 'ring' of the classically- trained voice, also called the 'singer's formant', which, rather than volume alone, enables a singer to be heard over a large orchestra). Higher pitches were very difficult for the early machines. Their narrow recording range fits the tenor voice much better, and the resultant more real sound no doubt helped to account for the huge success of Gaisberg's recordings of Caruso in April 1902.

Since Moreschi's own voice was a soprano, one might have feared the worst for the results, but he was fortunate in that acoustically the castrato voice differs radically from the female or boy soprano (and, incidentally, from any type of counter-tenor). A few moments listening to his singing reveals that in terms of vocal technique the castrato soprano was effectively a tenor singing 'impossibly' high, and doing so in a way that corresponds closely with present-day conceptions of how tenors sang in the period before the arrival of Duprez. In modern vocal pedagogy it is generally (though not universally – hardly anything in the teaching of singing is!) acknowledged that a tenor will sing in 'chest' voice to around the C# or D just above 'middle C', at which point he enters a part of the voice called the *passagio* or 'passage'. This is where he leaves the level of his ordinary speaking 'chest' voice, and moves into higher pitches which in speech would only be used for, say, calling across a room, or shouting across a football pitch. To sing successfully in this range clearly requires technical skill, since it is hardly advisable to shout for half an opera! It was Duprez who developed a particular technique for negotiating this 'zone' of the voice, though his is by no means the only method, let alone the safest.

Moreschi's 'chest' voice therefore operates to the C# or D an octave higher than a tenor, beyond which he uses a lighter though still powerful register, which is much more 'falsetto' in quality. He does not attempt to continue the chest voice into this higher register – this is possible for a tenor, but for a castrato may never have been so (for reasons which are not, and maybe never can be, understood). However, his technique is completely in accord with the writings of such noted authorities as the castrato singer and teacher Pier Francesco Tosi, whose *Riflessioni sul Canto Figurato* (translated into English (1743) by John Galliard as 'Observations on the Florid Song') had been published as long ago as 1723. Moreschi, however, despite Tosi and many others' exhortations to the contrary, makes remarkably little effort to smooth over the 'break' between the two registers. In this, though, he is doing no worse than many other famous singers of his time (and ours), especially women. His use of a lighter registration in the high range probably explains the concerns of the Sistine authorities over heavier style of tenor and bass singing which became so popular from the 1840s onwards (see above pp 53-54), and which could have caused balance problems. Had Moreschi been an alto castrato, he would have sounded like a baritone or bass singing 'an octave too high'.

That Moreschi sang in his modal, speaking voice an octave above middle C helps explain the castrati's legendary ability to sing extraordinarily long phrases in a single breath, since the modal voice needs less breath than falsetto. However skilful their emulation of the castrato manner and style of singing, this is one way in which modern counter-tenors cannot imitate them. If a counter-tenor attempts to sing high in his speaking, chest voice, he will eventually ruin the lower extension he has in his falsetto range, which is after all every bit as important as singing high, and is frequently only acquired by much practice. (I have heard several recordings of male sopranos who are apparently endocrinological castrati, suffering from congenital disorders such as Kallmann's syndrome; they all sound far more like ordinary falsettists than like Moreschi, none of them having his strong and extensive chest register). The thrilling sound of the modern operatic tenor is, however, achieved by taking the chest voice up to an octave above normal speaking range. If done well, this is not a matter of 'forcing', but it does account for many tenors losing most or all ability to sing in falsetto. For female sopranos (at least those needing to sing in the classical idiom) it is also technical suicide to sing more than a few semitones above middle C in the chest register, and so they also require more breath than the castrati did to sing in this pitch area.

As to the quality of Moreschi's singing on the recordings, it is certainly true that he sounds nervous on some of the tracks from the 1902 sessions, even making mistakes in a well-known solo like the *Crucifixus* from Rossini's *Petite Messe solennelle*. It should be remembered that recording was by no means the comparatively everyday experience it is today, and the oddness of the situation would have contributed to his uncertainty, as would the physical difficulties inherent in singing for the recording equipment of the day outlined above. Moreschi has been castigated for his failings in this and other respects. I might point out that Caruso's first recordings are also not without mistakes, and he has largely escaped similar critical condemnation. I well remember my own uncertainties when recording for the first time, even though, unlike Moreschi, I had the technological advantage of multiple retakes being available.

If this factor is taken into consideration, Moreschi's achievement becomes all the more remarkable. As the final survivor of a distinguished race of singers, and under artistic pressure from reforming forces beyond his control, it is a testament to his strength of character (no doubt forged during his schooldays) that he made the recordings at all. He would hardly have been personally encouraged to do so by the new Vatican regime, but surely realised that this was something of a last chance for the now old-fashioned and outlawed repertoire which had formed the core of his performing life, and was as a result very dear to him.

This love for what he is singing is audible in every note, however sentimental his style or quirky his technique may sound to some ears. It is, incidentally, revelatory to listen to the recordings with the addition of a little echo, imitating the Sistine Chapel's own acoustic: virtually all trace of the unsteadiness for which Moreschi has been frequently criticised disappears. It also helps to explain the oddest feature of his singing, a frequent addition of rapid *acciaccature* ('crushed notes') an octave below the written note. This seems to have been used as a way of adding richer low undertones to his high range, and would have worked particularly well in a generously echoing space.

As far as is known, there exist 17 recordings of Moreschi, either as soloist or member of an ensemble. These conveniently fall into three categories: solo song, 19th century sacred and 'early' sacred. (I have used the first category very loosely, including in it both the Bach/Gounod *Ave Maria* and Rossini *Crucifixus*, since neither, though having sacred texts, was intended for liturgical use.)

I make no apology for first discussing Gounod's adaptation of the First Prelude from Bach's 'Well-Tempered Klavier,', Book 1.

Of the solo works Moreschi recorded, it is far and away the best-known, and, since it had first appeared in 1859, I have already hazarded that it may have been sung by Alessandro during his childhood. To Anglo-Saxon non-Catholic ears this version of the most famous of prayers to the Virgin Mary may seem overloaded with sentiment, but Moreschi certainly 'goes for it' in his interpretation. To echo Mrs de Hegemann-Lindencrone there really is 'a tear' in virtually every note, but if one can live with that (I certainly can) and appreciate other stylistic differences from a modern, cooler approach, his singing is enormously affecting and totally genuine. He is very skilful in his varied use of vibrato, usually slight, but breaking out with great emotion on the phrase *ora pro nobis* ('pray for us') – this was clearly a man who knew what he was about, both interpretatively and technically. He uses slightly modified vowels on certain high pitches, which is a frequently-advised technique for avoiding an over-wide, blatant sound quality, and was also careful to husband his voice when needful: the climactic high B is taken gently and carefully. By this time it was probably at or very near the top of his voice, since it sounds very pure and falsetto-like; the descending notes following it are much more emotionally sung.

The rapid scoops up and down which Moreschi frequently uses in this piece (and throughout his recordings) are not merely sentimental, nor, *pace* some other commentators, do I think them to be evidence of poor technique: they are an integral part of his interpretative equipment, and are particularly effective when used with such words as *Maria* and *mulieribus*. Moreover, these scooping glissandi are very similar to techniques used by other contemporary singers and instrumentalists, as can be heard in early Elgar recordings, for example. He also makes some use of a intrusive 'h' in legato phrases – like so many other devices used by singers, this can become annoying if used to excess (the famous tenor Beniamino Gigli was perhaps the greatest over-exploiter of this 'sobbing' mannerism), while the flickering mordent-like ornament on the last 'Amen' is straight from his traditional manner of singing plainsong. There are some details of performance practice here to which we might be allergic today, but, in these days of 'historically informed performance' we should perhaps not be choosy as to which periods of music we wish to be historically informed about and which not.

The two items by Francesco Paolo Tosti (1846-1916) are in a similar sentimental vein and both have texts of a suitably spiritual nature. Even if Moreschi had retained the technical equipment to sing Gounod's 'Jewel Song' in 1904, which there is good reason to doubt, the recording and therefore permanent public record of such avowedly secular (not to mention sexually ambiguous) carryings-on would hardly have been thought becoming in a Papal singer. *Ideale* was the only 7" disc made by Moreschi, and may perhaps have been something of a 'try-out'. Tosti, who in 1880 became singing master to the British royal family, was an enormously popular composer of songs suitable for the salon and the drawing-room, and *Ideale* is just the sort of piece with which Moreschi would have entertained audiences in fashionable Roman *salotti* during his earlier career. He sings it with an almost artless simplicity, just as it should be. A sentimental ballad doesn't require sentimental performance. For a man whose personal life may have been rather unsatisfactory, singing these lines had special resonance: 'My solitary room was filled with your splendour . . . and on that day I forgot every trouble and every cross of this earth'. The hearty and spontaneous applause he receives from his colleagues present in the room when the song was recorded is strangely moving, but may also have helped to impress on Gaisberg that the whole enterprise was worthwhile. Moreschi is also careful not to over-egg the piety of the text of *Preghiera* ('Prayer') by indulging in vocal effects – this is essentially a very simple song with a regularly pulsing chordal accompaniment.

Simple songs are often the hardest to perform well, and Alessandro is very sensible in leaving Tosti's melody largely to speak for itself, while adding suitably expressive phrasing at such words as *'a te sospiro e piango'* ('I sigh and cry to Thee'). He tries too hard in the repeated invocations *'Signor, Pietà'* ('Lord, have mercy') that end the song, and in attempting to finish on a very quiet high G (never the easiest thing to do), his voice cracks for a moment.

It is worth mentioning that this is virtually the only fault in over 12 minutes continuous singing: no mean feat. This is the last of four successive matrix numbers (2182h to 2185h), the first tracks recorded for Darby in 1904, and one can almost sense that he was annoyed with himself for this tiny mistake, since the next take, the *Ave Maria* on matrix 2187h, has particular intensity.

The first of this group, Rossini's *Crucifixus,* is one of the finest of Moreschi's recordings, and this was again perhaps due to his desire to make up for earlier failings. It is the only piece he recorded twice, and the first version, which he made with Gaisberg in 1902, would in today's digital world have been delet-ed without a murmur; early recording masters were just too expensive to waste. Alessandro shows his inexperience: he starts well, but takes a wrong turning during the recapitulation of the main tune, going wrong and staying wrong for a couple of bars, to particularly cacophonic effect. This momentary failure of concentration clearly threw him for the rest of the take, since he makes an unusually wavering entry on one of the final phrases. The 1904 version comes from another planet: Moreschi is con-fident, and his inherently, rather than overtly, emotive performance safely negotiates any dangers of the religiose sentimentality of which (I think quite unjustifiably) the whole of Rossini's *Petite Messe solennelle* is sometimes accused. The 19th-century liturgical items that Moreschi recorded also include two solos by very obscure 19th-century composers: Ignace Xavier Joseph Leybach (1817-1891, and spelt Leibach on the discs), a French pianist and

Rossini's *Petite Messe Solenelle* was one of the last works outside the Roman basilicas to have been written with castrati in mind. The second page of Rossini's autograph bears the remark 'Twelve singers of three sexes, men, women, and castrati will be sufficient for its performance. . . this little piece which is, alas, the last mortal sin of my old age.'

organist from Strasbourg, and Eugenio Terziani (1824-1889), a pupil of Giuseppe Baini. Neither Leybach's *Pie Jesu* nor Terziani's *Hostias et Preces* is music of high quality, repeating many standard mid-19th century musical gestures without particular inspiration (the latter, from a *Requiem,* had been written in memory of Vittorio Emmanuele II). That said, the Leybach piece was sufficiently highly regarded as recently as 1963 to be performed (by a tenor) at President Kennedy's funeral, and at least one Nocturne of his for piano solo is still in print. Stylistically both are almost indistinguishable from Tosi's drawing-room ballads, and so are just the sort of music abhorred by the Cecilianists, who would have also loathed their extended solo nature and the fact that they were accompanied by that secular horror, the piano. This is perhaps one reason why Moreschi's sings them so well, particularly the Terziani, in which he handles the high tessitura skilfully and produces some fine quiet singing. He also negotiates two phrases ending on upward leaps with complete aplomb – this sort of writing, though simple to the casual hearer, can be the stuff of singers' nightmares.

The anti-Cecilianist flavour of this repertoire can be savoured even more, if anything, in those numbers where Moreschi is joined by a chorus of other papal singers. The motet *Dominum Salvum Fac Pontificem Nostrum Leonem* ('Lord, save our Pope Leo') by Giovanni Aldega is so theatrical in flavour as to sound just like one of Capocci's *rifacimenti* of 19th-century opera. With Moreschi soaring very convincingly over the rather distant chorus (they were presumably standing quite some way from Gaisberg's three recording horns) we are in a world not so far from that of the famous *Miserere* in Verdi's *Il Trovatore.* The extract from the Gloria of Capocci's own *Mass of St Bonaventure* is in a similar vein. Moreschi is here joined by his tenor colleague Cesare Boezi, who is competent if rather wooden, and by the operatic bass Armando Dadò, whose phrasing is hardly that of a subtle artist. Though both his fellow soloists were using the modern 'robust' method of singing throughout their respective ranges, Moreschi more than holds his own.

This track is perhaps more notable for the quality of the choral singing, which is frankly dreadful, particularly the upper voices. If this was what Perosi had to put up with when he arrived at the Sistine Chapel, one can only sympathise with him. It must be said that, on the evidence of this and other tracks, his proposed exclusive use of boy singers could hardly have augured any better, since their contribution to the top lines is every bit as bad as the castrati who can be faintly heard supporting them; the latter are so wobbly that 'support' is hardly the appropriate word. This is horribly obvious at several points in the *Tui sunt coeli* by Johan Gustav Eduard Stehle (1839-1915), a 'rum-ti-tum' affair redolent of Salvation Army tambourines, and in a soggy version of Mozart's wonderful *Ave verum,* which is reduced to saccharine stodge of the worst kind. The performance is so bad as almost to bring down Mozart's tiny masterpiece to the distinctly average level of the setting of the same text by Salvatore Meluzzi, master of the choir of St Peter's in Moreschi's time, which the choir recorded on the same day. These tracks are exclusively choral, and I would like to think Moreschi had nothing to do with them. I should further wonder whether the travesty of the Mozart in particular didn't give Gaisberg good reason to doubt whether his trip to Rome had been worth the trouble.

Matters were little better in 1904, when Darby was forced to sit through some really nasty singing from the chorus sopranos

and altos in Emilio Calzanera's *Oremus Pro Pontifice Nostro Pio.*
There is one particularly embarrassing moment when the soprano
boys and then a single alto castrato, (probably Salvatori) perhaps
joined by one wavery boy alto, sing the text *et beneficet eum* ('and
let it favour him')[166] – the singing at this point does no-one any
favours, to say the least. This is a pity, since Moreschi enjoys himself
enormously, entering into the emotionally extravagant spirit of
this piece with the commitment of a true professional. It should be
remembered that the text of this work praises the man who had
recently signed a *motu proprio* bringing to an end the castrati's
350-year reign in the Sistine Chapel. Calzanera would hardly have
written this piece just for the recording, so Pius would have had to
sit through at least one public rendition. What the Pope would
have thought of the unashamedly operatic treatment of the text
can be well imagined – the words 'Cecilian' and 'Gregorian' hardly
spring to mind in describing its full-throated theatricality, with
Moreschi's soaring rendition serving to remind His Holiness only
too well of the extraordinary baby that was being thrown out along
with the bath-water of Sistine tradition. Calzanera had himself
been a bass in the Sistine choir since 1879, and it is as if both he
and Moreschi were saying to Perosi and the pontiff 'beat that with
a boy soprano if you can!' Perhaps the two reformers might have
done well to pause and consider the words of a falsettist colleague
of Moreschi, Giovanni Gavazzi, for all that he may indulge somewhat in hyperbole: 'Moreschi was the most evocative phenomenon
of his time, to which he gave unmatchable expression in the midst
of chaotic forms of art, where the most select classical music was
muddled with grotesqueries of the worst kind. One may well talk
of 'white voices',[167] but the term should not be used in the same
breath as perhaps the most beautiful voice with which nature chose
to enrich us by means of the human throat.'[168]

There remain the recordings of the most traditional Sistine
repertoire, though a Palestrina madrigal doesn't fit into this

sacred context. Conducted by Kanzler, a man devoted to Cecilianist reform, there is no ornamentation in this or the Victoria *Improperia*, but the performance is still loaded with Romantic mannerism, the use of *glissandi* being particularly noticeable – and a long way from the cleaner style to which we are accustomed nowadays. At least the solo quartet in *La cruda mia nemica* sound involved in the text, but they are by no means note perfect. At Moreschi's first entry something is clearly amiss, while his contralto colleague (I think Salvatori again, who seems to use only his 'chest' register) with none of Alessandro's penetrating tone quality, often sounds quite vague and wobbly. (Perhaps this is why Perosi let him stay on at the Sistine: if he were virtually inaudible his singing would hardly affect the timbre of the boy altos). The Victoria is heavy and slow by today's standards, but this would have suited the Sistine Chapel's echoing spaces much better than the acoustically dry salon where the recording was made.

Moreschi seems not a jot disturbed by the dead acoustic in which he was singing when it comes to the only track in which his voice is totally unsupported by any accompaniment. The section he sings from the plainsong Lamentations is above all a personal statement. As first soprano in the Sistine Chapel Choir for over 20 years, it had been his proud duty to begin the singing of this most solemn office of the church's year, the service of 'Tenebrae', commemorating that darkness which came over the face of the whole earth when the crucified Christ at last gave up the ghost. Moreschi again sings here with unfaltering directness, not giving a fig for the fact that he is using the by then illegal Medicean edition of the chant, the tradition of which dated back to the time of Palestrina and beyond. In this track we can also hear most clearly his use of the upwardly leaping *acciaccatura,* that 'attack so firm it achieves uncouthness' as Gounod termed it,[169] which seems strange to our ears, and for which Moreschi has been much criticised. The technique had long been used at the Sistine, having been described at some length by Baini in his published history of the choir's Gregorian practice - he terms it 'an impetuous aspiration . . . that simply cannot be written down . . .'[170] Moreschi achieves an authenticity of utterance derived from experience rather than scholarship. Furthermore, he must have known that this would in all probability be the last time he would ever perform this music, at least publicly, but he betrays no personal emotion and loads no false feeling onto Jeremiah's timeless text. The gentle fading away at the words 'Jerusalem, turn again to the Lord Thy God' provides a moving close, fitting in its simplicity, but is again the sign of man knowing his job, and doing it well.

The recordings made in 1902 and 1904 by the Gramophone Company are certainly precious historical documents giving a fascinating insight into the repertoire and performance practices, good and bad, of the papal singers of the period. But there were also remarkable omissions from these sessions. It is firstly odd that Baron Kanzler, rather than Perosi himself, took charge of the only Palestrina items recorded. Perhaps Perosi thought the choir were not yet capable of the type of rendition he preferred, and so sidestepped the 'touchstone' issue of whether he could produce a suitably Cecilianist rendering from them by only directing a piece in similar style by the much less known Ludovico da Viadana (1560-1627). As to those pieces, which Moreschi and his colleagues seem to have had a choice in recording, it is extraordinary that, while they included works by Meluzzi (in 1902) and Capocci (in 1904) from the other papal basilicas, they completely neglected their 'illustrious and honoured master', Domenico Mustafà, who, in May 1902 at least, was still technically their Perpetual Director. Was there some dispute between him and his choir which was never publicly discussed, or was it just thought politically inept to record his music at a troubled time in the Sistine's history? The greatest sadness, however, is that the famous Allegri

Miserere was not recorded. Again there may have been internal political reasons for this, but it is likely that Moreschi by this date had himself begun to feel the effects of aging, and could no longer sustain the high tessitura of the solo soprano part for the required length of time (some 10 minutes).[171] With the technology available today, I hope some musically-gifted manipulator of computer software will be moved to attempt a digital reconstruction of Moreschi performing this work – an exciting prospect.

From the above comments I think it is clear that I am enthusiastic about Moreschi's voice and his singing, and also retain a sneaking liking for much of the 19th-century music he so obviously enjoyed performing – I certainly prefer it to the worthy Cecilianist repertoire. Most recent commentators have been negative, even dismissive, though Robert Donington's remarks are interestingly positive: 'a very remarkable experience . . . contrary to our modern expectation . . . nothing feminine, still less effeminate, in this voice of masculine weight and silky power.'[172] I particularly like that last phrase, repeated hearings of Moreschi having made me like him more as a singer, whilst admitting that my earliest reaction was one of surprise as well as curiosity. I have never felt the repulsion of some, who are often (rightly) also indignant, even disgusted, at the barbarity of castration as a whole. Unavoidably imbued as we are with the moral attitudes of today, it is hard to know how we might have reacted 100 or even 300 years ago, when, at the sound of a castrato's voice, opera houses would echo to the cry: 'Long live the knife'.

Notes

1 V L Bullough, 'Eunuchs in History and Society', S Tougher (ed), *Eunuchs in Antiquity and Beyond* (London: 2002), p 6

2 Tougher, p 2

3 G C Stent in his article *Chinese Eunuchs* in *Journal of the North-China Branch of the Royal Asiatic Society,* 9 (1877) pp 143-184, referred to by Bullough, states that in several years he saw only one failure.

4 Petronius *Satyricon,* tr Arrowsmith, (New York: 1987) 4.23,36

5 both quotations from D'Ancillon *Traité des Eunuques* (Amsterdam: 1707) p 11, as translated by Buning, who supplies much useful additional information.

6 see Witt, R: 'The Other Castrati' in Tougher, p 241-2

7 J-P Migne (ed) *Patrologia Graeca*, (Paris:1865) vol 137, p532

8 'De dioecesana synodo', (Rome: 1783), p 293

9 A Milner, 'The Sacred Capons', *Musical Times*, vol 114, p 250-252

10 A Newcomb, *The Madrigal in Ferrara 1579-1597* (Princeton: 1980), p 30-31

11 I Fenlon, *Music and Culture in Renaissance Italy* (Oxford: 2002), p 111

12 R Sherr, 'Guglielmo Gonzaga and the castrati', *Renaissance Quarterly*, 33 (1980), p 33-56

13 bull entitled *Cum pro nostro pastorali munere* from *Collectionis Bullarium brevium allorumque Diplomatum sacro sanctae Basilicae Vaticanae*, (Rome: 1752), iii, 172

14 Archivio Segreto Vaticano, Armadio XI n92, f152; see'Castrati della Cappella Pontificia' in P Levillani (ed) *Dizionario storico del papato* (Bompiani: 1996) vol 1, pp 270-72

15 unfortunately, no source for these colourful remarks has been identified

16 A. Theiner, *Acta Concilii Tridentium*, (Zagreb: 1874), ii, 122

17 J-J François de Lalande, *Voyage d'un François en Italie*, (Venice/Paris: 1769), VI, p 348

18 W L Weckerlin *Chronologien* (Frankfurt: 1779-81), I, p 174

19 original text quoted in J Rosselli *The Castrati as a Professional Group and a Social Phenomenon, 1550-1850*, p154, n47 *Acta Musicologica*, LX (Basel: 1988) pp 143-179

20 E. Faustini-Fassini, *Gli astri maggiori del bel canto napoletano, Note d'archivo*, 15, (1938), p 12

21 As reported by Milner [see note 9]. Another version of the story tells it of the famous 17th century castrato Domenico Cortona.

22 This is referred to in G Gullo, 'La Fabbrica degli Angeli', *Hortus Musicus*, 9 (January – March 2002), p53, n 10. Gullo, however, suggests that Moreschi, not least because of his small stature, was a congenital castrato of some sort. I wholly disagree with this, since photographic evidence shows that he was only of comparatively small stature during approximate ly the last 20 years of his life.

23 in some sources spelled *diocesana*

24 Casanova: *Memoirs*; tr Arthur Machen, with additional tr by Arthur Symons, (London: 1894), Vol 4c, Ch 10; complete text available at www.gutenberg.net

25 P Scholes (ed), *Dr Burney's Musical Tours in Europe* (London: 1959); Vol 1, p 247

26 Hector Berlioz, *Les Soirées de l'Orchestre*, sixième soirée, (Paris: 1852), section entitiled *Étude astronomique, révolution du ténor autour du public*

27 mea culpa, but not only mine

28 sometimes spelt as two words, thus: 'Monte Compatri'

29 There may be some confusion here: the detailed and carefully kept records of the parish church of the Annunziata in Montecompatri also record sever al children born to one Agostino Moreschi 'son of Luigi and of Rosa Pitolli', who married Victoria Ciuffa, and had at least four children between 1862 and 1867 – perhaps Alessandro had another older brother.

30 Haböck states that he is deriving his facts about Moreschi from direct conversation with the man himself.

31 The French soprano Caroline Miolan-Carvalho (also the first Marguerite in Gounod's opera *Faust*) gave the first public performance of the version of Gounod's work with this text on May 24 1859.

32 correspondence with G B Salvatori quoted in J K Law: 'Alessandro Moreschi Reconsidered: A Castrato on Records', *Opera Quarterly* vol 2, no 2, (Summer 1984), pp 1-12

33 Always considered a scourge of obscure Asiatic origin, cholera's true bacterial cause was only identified by the German physician Robert Koch in 1883.

34 in conversation with Franz Haböck, see pp 120-121

35 Frascati was a 'suburbicarian see' of Rome itself, its bishop being one of the eight cardinal-bishops; a famous incumbent was, Henry Stuart, Duke of York, brother of 'Bonnie Prince Charlie'.

36 this information has been gleaned from Jan Lahmeyer's wonderful website at www.library.uu.nl/wesp/populstat/populhome.html

37 "Se siete cattolici, dunque ringraziate il Cielo che il principato temporale sia finito; si è chiusa la più grande e vergognosa piaga della Religione cattolica nel mondo". Much fascinating information on this period in Italian history is provided online at www.cronologia.it

38 D Mack Smith, *Italy A modern History;* (Ann Arbor: 1959), p 96

39 The training of another young castrato, Costantino Maddalena (born in 1854), had been envisaged by the members of the Sistine in April 1870, but the fall of Rome to royal troops had prevented this, and nothing more is known of this young man: see Diario Sistino 285, f 46r

40 These were St Peter's, known as the 'Basilica Vaticana', master of music Salvatore Meluzzi (1813-1897), Santa Maria Maggiore, the 'Basilica Liberiana', master of music Settimo Battaglia (1815-1891), and San Giovanni Laterano, the 'Basilica Lateranense', master of music Gaetano Capocci (1811-1898). The Lateran is the Pope's seat as 'Bishop of Rome'.

41 It was full to overflowing by the mid-19th century, a situation that was not resolved because of the turmoil surrounding the fall of the Papal States in 1870.

42 Alberto de Angelis, *La Musica a Roma nel secolo XIX*, (Rome: 1935), p 93

43 L de Hegemann-Lindencrone, *The Sunny Side of Diplomatic Life*, (New York: 1914), p 117

44 It is noteworthy that Mrs Hegemann-Lindencrone, like the recording engineer Fred Gaisberg some 30 years later, greatly over-estimated Moreschi's age. This was a frequent occurrence with castrati, as they possessed an unusual skin quality, a result of their anomalous physiology.

45 de Hegemann-Lindencrone, p 118-119, dated 1883

46 Vatican Library, Diario Sistino 272, f 13r. The *diario* was a record of all events of significance in the life of the Chapel – truly a 'daily' book, as the word literally means. Hereafter 'DS'.

47 de Hegemann-Lindencrone, p 118

48 Luigi Devoti, 'Alessandro Moreschi detto "L'angelo di Roma" 1858-1922', in R Lefevre and A Morelli (eds) *Musica e musicisti nel Lazio* (Rome: 1985), p 467

49 Alessandro Gabrielli, 'Riassunto delle conversazioni sulla storia delle cappelle musicali romane', *Rassegna Dorica,* x (1938-1939), p 255; Gabrielli was a falsettist in the Sistine Chapel choir and a younger colleague of Moreschi.

50 Robert Buning, *Alessandro Moreschi and the Castrato Voice* (M Mus, Boston: 1990) p122; Buning's translation.

51 Though he had been presented with a copy at the time of publication, the then Director of the Sistine Choir, Giuseppe Baini (1775–1844), had not been keen on Beethoven's music, and, moreover the libertarian Beethoven had certainly been *persona non grata* with the extremely conservative Vatican hierarchy of the day. The oratorio dates from 1803 and is rarely performed today. It shows the influence of Beethoven's older contemporary Salieri (the supposed nemesis of Mozart) and the composer himself was apparently dissatisfied with the work.

52 F Haböck, *Die Kastraten und ihre Gesangskunst* (Berlin: 1927), p 206

53 Gabrielli, Riassunto, p 239

54 DS 263, ff 90r-92v, dated 24 August 1847

55 DS 233, f 28r – an annotation made in 1817.

56 DS 235, f 30r

57 both quotations from A C Jemolo, *Church and State in Italy 1850-1950*, tr David Moore (Oxford: 1960), p 6

58 R. de Cesare, *The Last Days of Papal Rome*, abridged and tr Helen Zimmein (London: 1909), preface, p ix

59 Gabrieli, Riassunto, p 254

60 DS 265, f 23v

61 this title is sometimes given as *Direttore dei Concerti*, but *concerto* here means group of soloists set against the *ripieno* full choir, and has, I believe no connotations of 'concert' in the modern sense.

62 see a letter from the papal major-domo's office dated January 2 1878, and recorded in DS 287, f 16

63 translated from DS 289, f 5 ff

64 Gabrielli, Riassunto, p 253

65 The relationship between *fauxbourdon* and the later *falsobordone* is a complex one, but both involved some form of descanting, harmonic or melodic, against a pre-existing melody; see B Trowell, 'Fauxbourdon' in *The New Grove Dictionary of Music and Musicians,* ed S Sadie and R Tyrell (London:2001), vol 8, pp 614-620; and M C Bradshaw, 'Falsobordone' in the same publication vol 8, pp 538-539.

66 This version is best known from the recording made by the choir of King's College, Cambridge in 1963 . It should also be pointed out that the famous 'high C' for the solo soprano did not originate with this version: though 19th-century scores only have high G, we have it from no less an authority than Mendelssohn that the Sistine choir traditionally performed this work at a pitch a 3rd or 4th higher than that of the score. He also notates an ornamented version at high pitch in a letter dated June 16 1831, as printed in the second edition of his *Letters from Italy and Switzerland*, trs Lady Wallace; London, 1862 p177-178. The absolute pitch of performance, after some 300 years of Roman eclecticism, had been fixed at a conference held in Vienna in 1885 at A432-435 Hz, the French 'dia pason normal'.

67 described in the Annuaire Pontifical Catholique for 1899, p377; curiously the French edition of the official calendar of the church's year and 'record of personnel' is often much more detailed than the original Italian edition

68 see www.cronistoria.it

69 DS 290, c 47r

70 by the publishers Manganelli

71 Otto Nicolai, 'Über die Sixtinische Kapelle in Rom', in G R Kruse (ed) *Musikalische Aufsätze* (Regensburg, Deutsche Musikbücherei, vol 10, no date), p 71

72 Nicolai, p74

73 DS 294, f 14r

74 Felix Mendelssohn Bartholdy, *Reisebriefe aus den Jahren 1803 bis 1832,* ed Paul Mendelssohn Bartholdy (Leipzig: 1869), p 143

75 de Hegemann-Lindencrone, p 184

76 then as now a luxurious establishment near the Piazza del Popolo

77 Devoti,p 468

78 ibid

79 DS 293, f 4v

80 Alfredo De Angelis, *Domenico Mustafa, La cappella Sistina e la Società Musicale Romana* (Bologna:1926), p 48. De Angelis also wrote for the Roman newspaper *La Tribuna* and took a great interest in the Sistine Chapel Choir. Incidentally, there seems little foundation for the story that, the Vatican authorities considered approaching Franz Liszt, who was living in Rome from 1861 to 1869 to take up the post of Director – his name never appears in any Sistine-related document.

81 DS 297, ff 12v-13

82 DS 293, ff 12-13v

83 DS 293, f 4v

84 Vatican Library, Fondo Cappella Sistina 642, p 474-478

85 DS 293, f 7

86 DS 294, ff 9v-10v

87 I have read one unsubstantiated report that a copy of Mustafá's version was found in Moreschi's papers after his death.

88 This manuscript is now number 375 in the Fondo Cappella Sistina of the Vatican Library.

89 DS 294, f 18

90 P F Saverio, *Brevi Cenni Storici della Miracolosa Immagine di Maria S{antis}sima del Castagno,* (Rome: 1892), p 46-47

91 online at http://www.papalencyclicals.net

92 *Annus qui hunc,* Chapter 1, paragraph 2

93 *Musica Divina,* Introduction p XIX

94 *Musica Sacra* VII, (Regensburg:1880), p 75

95 *Ordinatio quoad sacram musica,m* Actae Sanctae Sedis, vol XVII p340 ff

96 Cardinal Pecci died on the 8th.

97 Dom Pierre Combe, *Histoire de la Restauration du Chant Grégorien d'après des Documents Inédits,* (Solesmes: 1969), p 150; (The Catholic University of America Press).

98 Alfredo de Angelis, *La Musica a Roma nel secolo XIX* (Rome:1935), p 90

99 Ssee for example his article 'Musica alla Sistina e al Seminario Vaticano', *Civilta Cattolica* 4 April 1891, p 93 ff

100 DS 294, f 28v, dated 2 December 1892

101 DS 294, ff. 5-6, dated 13 January 1892

102 much information on Tebaldini is available online at www.tebaldini.it

103 DS 295, f 39r

104 A similar invitation to perform at an Exhibition of Arts and Sciences in London's Alexandra Palace in April 1894 was also turned down.

105 See footnote 58

106 DS 295, f 28

107 *L'Italia Reale* II, no 118 (Turin: 29/30 April 1891), p 1

108 letter dated 30 June 1894, recorded in DS 296, ff 24v-25

109 Acta Sanctae Sedis, vol XVII, p 340 ff

110 See *Dizionario degli Editori Italiani 1750-1930*, ed B M Antolini (Pisa: 2000). Manganelli published this piece in his first issue dated January 1 1878.

111 *Musica Sacra,* XVIII, (Milan: 6 May 1894), p 52-54

112 *La Voce della Verità,* XXV (Rome:March 5 1895) p 3, n 53

113 DS 298, ff 24-25v, 31-32

114 *Musica Sacra,* XX, p40 (Milan: 15 March 1896)

115 DS 298, f 10v

116 DS 298, ff 35r-36

117 This is recorded in the Sistine Diary for 1898.

118 from DS 1898, see Mario Rinaldi *Perosi* (Rome: 1967), p 111

119 reported in Rinaldi, p 114

120 De Angelis, *Mustafà,* p 72

121 De Angelis, *Mustafà,* p74 ff

122 De Angelis, *Mustafà,* p 74

123 De Angelis, *Mustafà,* p 77

124 Haböck, p204 describes Christmas madrigal concerts given by Sistine singers.

125 see www.lasalle.org

126 Devoti, p 465

127 Reported in De Angelis' biography of Mustafà, p 175.

128 See *L'Opinione, Gazzetta di Roma* dated 5 August 1900

129 The edition of *La Nazione* dated 3-4 August 1900 also mentions the Requiems by Verdi and Cherubini having been considered for performance at the king's funeral – either would have been a huge undertaking, especially considering the limited timescale involved. I have also seen it reported, online and without reference, that Moreschi sang some of the Seraph's music from 'Christ on the Mount of Olives' during the funeral service.

130 De Angelis, *Mustafà,* p 80, n 1

131 referred to in Gabrielli, Riassunto *Riassunto*

132 De Angelis, *Mustafà,* p 79

133 Rinaldi, *Perosi,* p155

134 Both quotations are from the satirical journal *Il Travaso delle Idee* (Rome: 31 May 1902)

135 Gaisberg's version of how Caruso came to be recorded, namely only through his paying Caruso's fee, his superiors in London having described it as 'exorbitant' has recently been shown to be false: see J R Bolig: *Caruso Records* (Mainspring Press, Highlands Ranch, Colorado: 2002), p 3.

136 He eventually relented on 5 February 1903, recording an apostolic blessing and intoning the *Ave Maria*. Pope Leo thus came to be one of the earliest-born humans (1810) ever to have been recorded – perhaps the very earliest. It should also be pointed out that he does of course sing the *Ave Maria*, rather than merely saying it.

137 It is no doubt this phrase that has given rise to the frequently repeated erroneous statement that Moreschi was 'Director of the Sistine Chapel Choir'. He was never more than *Direttore dei concertisti* (see p 69), though he did direct the members of the choir on some of the recordings .

138 F Gaisberg 'Notes from my Diary, Recording of Actual Performances' *Gramophone,* xxii, no 256, (September 1944), p 43

139 'The Fred Gaisberg Diaries', *The Talking Machine Review,* 63/64 (Bournemouth: 1981), p 1765 ff

140 or, at least, seven survive

141 *La Tribuna,* 28 December 1902; see also De Angelis, *Mustafà,* p 79-80 and p 175, n 6

142 see Buning p103; and P Barbier, *The World of the Castrati,* tr M Crosland (London:1996), p 238

143 Rinaldi, *Perosi,* p 158

144 R Hayburn, *Papal Legislation on Sacred Music 95AD to 1977AD,* (Collegeville, Minnesota: 1979), p212-219

145 For the text of this letter see online at http://www.adoremus.org/MotuProprio.html#anchor883761

146 The actual anniversary of Gregory's death was on 12 March, which fell during Lent that year – not a suitable time liturgically for celebrations..

147 Haböck, p 209; he gives no source for these observations, but I have found no other that contradicts them. It should be perhaps remembered that Pius X was later canonized.

148 See J Wolfson, notes to 'Alessandro Moreschi, the Last Castrato, the Complete Vatican Recordings', Opal CD 9823, (Wadhurst: 1987).

149 In 1967, Mancini, then 76 years old, recorded a long interview, published in the series of recordings *Le Voci di Roma – primo volume*; record no TIMA37, Edizioni del Timaclub, 1981. I am indebted to Robert Buning for his remarks on Mancini's singing, and his excellent translation of the interview, which includes, as he puts it, 'some tidying up'. I have translated a few extra passages and altered a few words here and there.

150 His privately made recording of the 'Bach/Gounod' Ave Maria is in E flat, which takes him from b flat to g": high for a falsettist, but not extraordinarily so.

151 It is by no means impossible to imitate the timbre of a castrato. I have heard it most convincingly done by a tenor, though I'm not sure he would have wished to continue the attempt for long.

152 De Angelis, *Mustafà,* p 175

153 M Rinaldi; 'Un Singolare schema per la riforma della Liturgia della Messa di Lorenzo Perosi' *Testimonianze, Studi e Ricerche in Onore di Guido M. Gatti (1892-1973)* Quadrivium XIV (1973)

154 This is odd, in the light of Moreschi's performances of Beethoven and Gounod noted earlier.

155 Haböck, pp 207-8; I have reordered his remarks somewhat.

156 quoted in Devoti pp 472-3

157 Gabrielli, p 256

158 I consulted a copy of this document in the Biblioteca Vaticana. It bears neither a publishing date, nor publisher's colophon.

159 now sadly replaced by a 60s apartment block

160 *Il Giornale d'Italia* 22 April 1922, p 6

161 *Il Giornale d'Italia* 30 April, p 2

162 for example *Il Corriere della Sera,* 30 April 1922, p 7, and *La Tribuna* same date, p 5

163 Situated at n° 2, Riquadro 31/bis.

164 See notes 150 and 151

165 This page is reproduced in Alan Kendall, *Rossini* (London: 1992), p 211

166 I think this text is correct: the singers' diction is as bad as their singing.

167 This was, and still is, the usual Italian term for boy soprano, but perhaps in using such a term one should not forget as well the overtones of pre-pubescence, and of purity in more senses than one. The phrase has also been used as a euphemism for 'castrato', and as a (hopefully preferably inaccurate) description of the counter-tenor voice.

168 Devoti, p 466

169 Charles Gounod, *Mémoires d'un Artiste* (Paris: 1896), p 99

170 Giuseppe Baini, 'Delle regole circa il modo di cantare le lezioni, le lamentazioni ed I capitoli (Rome: 1806), published in J A de la Fage *Essais de diphthérographie musicale ...* (Paris: 1864), p 462

171 Ben Byram-Wigfield recommends a performing time of a little over eight minutes (see note 70 above), but some recordings are nearer 15.

172 R Donington, *Performer's Guide to Baroque Music* (London: 1973), p73

Chronology

Year	Age	Life
1858		11 November: Alessandro Moreschi born in Montecompatri.
1867	8	Cholera outbreak in Colli Romani region – possible date for Moreschi's castration.
1871	12	Admitted to the choir-school of San Salvatore in Lauro.
1873	14	Becomes *primo soprano* in the choir of San Giovanni Laterano.
1878	19	Death of Pope Pius IX.
1881	22	Mustafà becomes *Direttore perpetuo* of the Sistine choir.
1883	24	22 March: admitted to the choir of the Sistine Chapel.
1884	25	Congregation of sacred rites officially recognises Cecilianist movement.

Chronology

Year	History	Culture
1858	Dissolution of English East India Company. At Lourdes, apparition of Virgin Mary.	Jacques Offenbach, *Orpheus in the Underworld.*
1867	US purchase Alaska from Russia. Joseph Lister introduces antiseptic surgery.	Giuseppe Verdi, *Don Carlos.* Johann Strauss, *The Blue Danube.* Marx, *Das Kapital.* Henrik Ibsen, *Peer Gynt.*
1871	William I proclaimed German emperor. In Africa, H M Stanley finds D Livingston at Ujiji.	Verdi, *Aïda.* Carroll, *Through the Looking-Glass.*
1873	In Spain, Amadeo I abdicates; republic proclaimed. Great Depression (until 1896).	Arthur Rimbaud, *A Season in Hell.* Claude Monet, *Impression: soleil levant*
1878	Congress of Berlin resolves Balkan crisis: In London, electric street lighting.	Tchaikovsky, *Swan Lake.*
1881	In Russia, Alexander II assassinated. In eastern Europe, Jewish pogroms.	Jacques Offenbach, *The Tales of Hoffmann.* Henry James, *Portrait of Lady.* Ibsen, *Ghosts*
1883	Jewish immigration to Palestine (Rothschild Colonies). Germany acquires southwest Africa. In Chicago, world's first skyscraper built.	Antonín Dvorák, *Stabat Mater.* Robert Louis Stevenson, *Treasure Island.*
1884	Berlin Conference to mediate European claims in Africa (until 1885). In Mexico, Porfirio Diaz becomes president (until 1911).	Mark Twain, *Huckleberry Finn.* Georges Seurat, *Une Baignade, Asnières.*

Year	Age	Life
1891	32	Becomes *segretario-puntatore* of the Sistine choir; 7 March: introduction of new Constitution for the choir.
1892	33	Becomes *maestro pro tempore*; 21 August: travels to Montecompatri to perform at 25th anniversary celebrations of the town's deliverance from cholera by of the Madonna del Castagno.
1894	35	Sistine Chapel choir performs at a tercentenary concert in commemoration of Palestrina.
1896	37	Moreschi is granted official leave to become a member of the choirs of St Peter's and St John Lateran as well as the Sistine Chapel; the Sistine choir performs at an international congress in Arezzo celebrating the 900th anniversary of the famous theorist Guido d'Arezzo.
1898	39/40	March: Mustafà decides to retire; 15 December: Lorenzo Perosi appointed joint *Direttore perpetuo* of the Sistine choir.
1900	41	9 August: Moreschi performs at the funeral of King Umberto I.
1902	43	3 February: Perosi obtains a papal injunction banning further recruitment of castrati to the Sistine choir – Mustafà resigns as *Direttore perpetuo*; 3-5 April: Moreschi makes his first recordings for Fred Gaisberg.
1903	44/45	20 July: death of Pope Leo XIII; 4 August: succeeded by Giuseppe Sarto, who takes the title of Pius X; 22nd November, Pope Pius X issues *motu proprio* entitled *Tra le sollecitudine*, reforming music in the Catholic church.
1904	45/46	April: Moreschi makes his second set of recordings; November: he begins teaching Domenico Mancini.

Year	History	Culture
1891	Building of Trans-Siberian railway begins. Shearers' strike in Australia.	Tchaikovsky, *The Nutcracker*. Oscar Wilde, *The Picture of Dorian Gray*. Henri Toulouse-Lautrec, *Le bal du Moulin-Rouge*.
1892	Panama scandal: F. de Lesseps is accused of corruption. Charles Cross discovers viscose. Rudolf Diesel patents the internal combustion engine.	Claude Monet begins with series of pictures of Rouen Cathedral (-1895). M Maesterlinck, *Pelléas et Mélisande,* with C Debussy's music.
1894	In France, Alfred Dreyfus convicted of treason. In Russia, Nicholas II becomes Tsar (until 1917). Sino-Japanese War (until 1895).	Claude Debussy, *L'Après-midi d'un Faune*. Gabriele d'Annuzio, *Il trionfo della morte*. Kipling, *The Jungle Book*. G B Shaw, *Arms and Man*.
1896	Theodore Herzl founds Zionism. First Olympic Games of the modern era held in Athens. Antoine (Henri) Becquerel discovers radioactivity of uranium.	Giacomo Puccini, *La Bohème*. Thomas Hardy, *Jude the Obscure*.
1898	Spanish-American War: Spain loses Cuba, Puerto Rico and the Philippines. Britain conquers Sudan.	Henry James, *The Turn of the Screw*. H G Wells, *The War of the Worlds*. Zola, *J'Accuse*. Auguste Rodin, *The Kiss*.
1900	In China, Boxer Rebellion (until 1901). Aspirin introduced. First Zeppelin flight.	Puccini, *Tosca*. Conrad, *Lord Jim*. Sigmund Freud, *The Interpretation of Dreams*.
1902	End of Boer War. Anglo-Japanese alliance.	Scott Joplin, *The Entertainer.* Arthur Conan Doyle, *The Hound of the Baskervilles*. Conrad, *The Heart of Darkness*. André Gide, *L'Immoraliste*. Claude Monet, *Waterloo Bridge*
1903	In Britain, suffragette movement begins. Panama Canal Zone granted to US to build and manage waterway. Wright Brothers' first flight.	Henry James, *The Ambassadors*. Antonio Gaudi begins work on upper transept of Sagrada Familia church in Barcelona. G B Shaw, *Man and Superman*
1904	France and Britain sign Entente Cordiale. Russo-Japanese War. Photoelectric cell invented.	Puccini, *Madama Butterfly*. Jack London, *The Sea Wolf*. J M Barrie, *Peter Pan*. Chekhov, *The Cherry Orchard*.

Year	Age	Life
1912	53	Death of Mustafà.
1913	54	22 March: Moreschi qualifies for his pension.
1914	55	April: interviewed by Austrian musicologist Franz Haböck
1919	60	12 March: Moreschi's former colleague Vincenzo Sebastianelli dies – Alessandro becomes truly 'The Last Castrato'; around Easter he falls ill
1922	63	21 April: death of Alessandro Moreschi

Year	History	Culture
1912	Titanic sinks. Dr Sun Yat-sen establishes Republic of China. Stainless steel invented.	Arnold Schoenberg, *Pierrot lunaire*. Carl Jung, *The Psychology of the Unconscious*. Bertrand Russell, *The Problems of Philosophy*.
1913	In US, Woodrow Wilson becomes president (until 1921). Hans Geiger invents Geiger counter.	Stravinsky, *The Rite of Spring*. Guillaume Apollinaire, *Les peintres cubistes*. D H Lawrence, *Sons and Lovers*. Marcel Proust, *A la recherche du temps perdu* (until 1927).
1914	28 June: Archduke Franz Ferdinand assassinated in Sarajevo. First World War begins. Panama Canal opens.	James Joyce, *The Dubliners*. Ezra Pound, *Des Imagistes*.
1919	Treaty of Versailles. In US, pro-hibition begins. Irish Civil War (until 1921).	Franz Kafka, *In the Penal Colony*. J M Keynes, *The Economic Consequences of the Peace*. The Bauhaus founded in Weimar. United Artists formed with Charlie Chaplin, Mary Pickford, Douglas Fairbanks and D W Grifith as partners.
1922	Soviet Union formed. Mussolini's fascists march on Rome.	T S Eliot, *The Waste Land*. Joyce, *Ulysses*.

Bibliography

general reference

The Catholic Encyclopedia (1911 edition online at
  www.newadvent.org/cathen)
The New Grove Dictionary of Music and Musicians, ed S Sadie and R
  Tyrell (London:2001)
Dizionario Universale della Musica e I Musicisti, ed A Basso (Turin:1988)

on castrati and castration

S Argentieri, 'Riflessioni sul destino di un evirato cantore' in S
  Cappelletto, *La Voce Perduta* (Turin:1995), pp 145-162; a useful
  article on psychological aspects of the castrato condition
P Barbier, *The World of the Castrati*, tr M Crosland (London:1996)
R Blanchard and R de Candé, *Dieux et Divas de l'Opéra* (Paris: 1986);
  very useful for its biographies of many singers, not just castrati
F Haböck, *Die Kastraten und ihre Gesangskunst* (Berlin: 1927); still a
  classic
A Heriot, *The Castrati in Opera* (London: new edition 1975); probably
  still the best book on the subject
C. D'Ancillon, *Traité des Eunuques* (Amsterdam:1707)
J S Jenkins, 'The Voice of the Castrato', *The Lancet*, 351 (1998)
  pp 1877-80
A Milner, 'The Sacred Capons', *Musical Times*, vol 114 (1973),
  pp 250-252
J Rosselli, 'The Castrati as a Professional Group and a Social
  Phenomenon, 1550-1850', *Acta Musicologica*, LX (Basel: 1988)
  pp 143-179; a first-rate article on castrato singers and their place
  in society
S Tougher (ed), *Eunuchs in Antiquity and Beyond* (London:2002); an
  up-to-the-minute digest of many aspects of 'eunuchry'

on the history of Italy, Rome, and the Papacy

J N D Kelly, *The Oxford Dictionary of Popes (Oxford: 1988)*; elegantly
written and packed with information

E Duffy, *Saints and Sinners* (Yale: 2002); described by *The Sunday
Telegraph* as a 'minor masterpiece'

R. de Cesare, *The Last Days of Papal Rome*, abridged and tr Helen
Zimmein (London: 1909)

M Clark, *Modern Italy* (Longman History of Italy, vol 7, London: 1984
– there is a revised edition, published in 1996)

A C Jemolo, *Church and State in Italy 1850-1950*, tr David Moore
(Oxford: 1960)

D Mack Smith, *Italy A modern History* (Ann Arbor: 1959; new edition:
1997); the classic text

Annuario Pontificio 1898-1923 (published annually in the Vatican
City, and its French version, the *Annuaire Pontifical Catholique*,
published in Paris)

www.catholic-hierarchy.org; most useful for tracing bishops, cardinals, etc

www.cronologia.it; a fascinating site, particularly useful for Italian
history

www.papalencyclicals.net; an extraordinary amount of work has gone
into the documentation on this site – highly recommended

on music in 19th-century Rome

A De Angelis, *Domenico Mustafa, La cappella Sistina e la Società Musicale
Romana* (Bologna:1926); still, I believe, the only full-scale study of
this important figure

A De Angelis, *La Musica a Roma nel secolo XIX*, (Rome: 1935)

Dom P Combe, *Histoire de la Restauration du Chant Grégorien d'après des
Documents Inédits*, (Solesmes: 1969); written from the Solesmes viewpoint, and extraordinarily detailed and thorough; an English translation was published in 2003 (The Catholic University of America Press)

V Donella, *La Musica in Chiesa*, (Bergamo: 1985)

A Gabrielli, 'Riassunto delle conversazioni sulla storia delle cappelle
musicali romane', *Rassegna Dorica*, x (1938-1939)

R Hayburn, *Papal Legislation on Sacred Music 95AD to 1977AD,*
(Collegeville, Minnesota: 1979),

A L de Hegemann-Lindencrone, *The Sunny Side of Diplomatic Life*, (New
York: 1914)

L M Kantner and A Pachovsky, *La Cappella Musicale Pontificia
nell'Ottocento*, (Rome: 1998); an indispensable work of reference

M Rinaldi, *Perosi* (Rome: 1967)

on Moreschi

R Buning, *Alessandro Moreschi and the Castrato Voice* (M Mus, Boston: 1990); a first-rate thesis

L Devoti, 'Alessandro Moreschi detto "L'angelo di Roma" 1858-1922', in R Lefevre and A Morelli (eds) *Musica e musicisti nel Lazio* (Rome: 1985)

E Scammell and J Wolfson, notes to 'Alessandro Moreschi, the Last Castrato, the Complete Vatican Recordings', Opal CD 9823, (Wadhurst: 1987)

on Montecompatri

M Buffi, *Monte Compatri e i Monticiani* (Monte Compatri: 2000); a very useful volume on the town, its history and its inhabitants

P F Saverio, *Brevi Cenni Storici della Miracolosa Immagine di Maria S{antis}sima del Castagno*, (Rome: 1892)

http://montecompatri.controluce.it the site of the town's monthly journal, also including much information on Montecompatri's history, traditions, and the like

Picture sources

The author and publishers wish to express their thanks to the following sources of illustrative material and/or permission to reproduce it. They will make proper acknowledgements in future editions in the event that any omissions have occurred

Akg-Images: pp. 8,12, 21, 22, 39, 52, 59, 72, 93, 117; Bridgeman Art Library: p. 16; Nicholas Clapton: p. 31; JKInc: p139; Lebrecht Music Collection: i, iii, x, 24, 41, 63, 120, 132, 133, 141; Mary Evans Picture Library: pp. 4, 108; Fratelli Alinari: pp.27, 29, 33, 47, 67, 79, 81, 82, 87, 91, 120; Scala Archives: p 36.

Index

Moreschi, 134, 139; and political upheavals, 51, 55–6, 58; Pope Pius IX's incarceration, 38, 39; Porta Santa Anna, 137; Portone di Bronzo, 137; protocol, 65; relations with Italian state, 46, 115; rumour of 'last castrato', 130–1; Sala Clementina, 99, 102

Velluti, Giovanni Battista, 21, 25

Venice, 6, 18, 25, 58, 97, 125; *ospedali*, 42; St Mark's, 112; Teatro la Fenice, 130

Verdi, Giuseppe, 42–3, 77, 82–3, 151

Verusio, Giovanni, 102

Viadana, Ludovico, 154

Victoria, Queen, 78

Victoria, Tomás Luis de, 7, 76, 96, 115, 129, 153

Vienna, 20, 58, 93, 135; Congress of, 34, 55

Vin Mariani, 78, 79

Vissani, Giosafat, 66, 130

Vittori, Loreto, 11

Vittorio Emmanuele II, King, 30, 35, 59, 114, 115, 150; troops entering Rome, 36–7

Vivaldi, Antonio, 95

Wagner, Richard, 60

Witt, Franz Xaver, 96–7, 103

women, 18, 43; repertoire, 83; on stage, 17–18, 20–1; voice registers, 144

World's Columbian Exhibition, 101